HEADWAY ENGLISH

by Howell Moses

Designed by
Lloyd Fishwick Associates

COLLINS EDUCATIONAL

Illustrations
Oena Armstrong pages 18, 24
Leonora Box pages 36-7, 48, 6 (top)
James Dodds pages 42, 56
Ray Fishwick pages 13, 19, 51, 55, 67, 70 73, 78
Mark Hudson page 60
Anita Jones pages 6 (bottom), 71, 89
David Mostyn pages 20, 94
Christina Newns pages 8, 32, 54, 61
Reg Piggott page 50
Michael Whittlesea pages 38, 63

The publishers would like to thank the following for permission to reproduce photographs:
Admiralty chart page 87
J Allan Cash Photolibrary page 16
BBC Hulton Picture Library page 12 (top), 34 (×2), 43 (bottom)
British Tourist Authority pages 13, 40-1, 62
Camera Press page 10 (bottom)
Cardiff Arms Park page 23
Civil Aviation Authority page 58
Clodwyn Climbing and Safety Equipment page 26
Colorsport page 22 (bottom right)
Dunlop Slazenger International Ltd page 4-5
Earthscape page 7
East Anglian Daily Times page 26 (×3)
Ray Fishwick pages 33, 91, 49 (bottom), 77 (middle), 76 (bottom)
Chris Gilbert page 76 (top)
Grenadier Guards page 64-5
The Guide Dogs for the Blind Association page 77 (top)
George Herringshaw & Associates page 22 (bottom left)
Alan Irvine page 74-5
Lyon Equipment page 29 (bottom)
Mansell Collection pages 35 (right), 43 (middle and top), 80-1, 86
By kind permission of His Grace the Duke of Marlborough page 35 (left)
Howell Moses page 83
David Munden Photography page 22 (top)
Emma Nicholson page 84 (bottom ×4)
Popperfoto page 52 (left)
Practical Gardening page 19
John Rae pages 12 (×3), 14 (×4), 31 (×3), 44, 46 (bottom), 49 (top), 52 (right), 55 (×2), 66 (×6), 76 (bottom) 82, 84, 93, 95
Rolls-Royce Motors Ltd pages 10-11 (top ×2)
Science Museum pages 46 (top), 47 (×4)
Sport and General page 23 (top)
Swiss National Tourist Office pages 25, 29 (top)
Topham Picture Library page 28
David Wilkinson page 68
The Zoological Society of London/Michael Lyster pages 17 (×2), 77 (bottom)

The author and publishers wish to thank the following copyright owners for permission to quote from copyright works:
page 20 'The Habits of the Hippopotamus' by Arthur Guiterman from **The Children's Book of Comic Verse** published by Pan Books
page 91 'Trees' by Sara Coldridge from **A Book of a Thousand Poems** published by Bell and Hyman Ltd

© 1986 Howell Moses
0 00 323002 3
Published by Collins Educational
8 Grafton Street, London W1X 3LA
Published 1986
Reprinted 1987

Printed in Great Britain by R. J. Acford, Chichester

Designed by Lloyd Fishwick Associates

CONTENTS

Anyone For Tennis?   4

Rolls Royce   10

The River Horse of Africa   16

Rugby — The Welsh Obsession   22

Check-Out 1 — Mountaineering   28

Winston Churchill   34

The Lake District   40

Cutty Sark   46

New Year Celebrations   52

Check-Out 2 — Radar   58

The British Grenadiers   64

The Father of the Modern Computer   68

The Buried City of Mount Vesuvius   74

Samuel Pepys   80

Check-Out 3 — Goodwin Sands   86

Final Check-Out   92

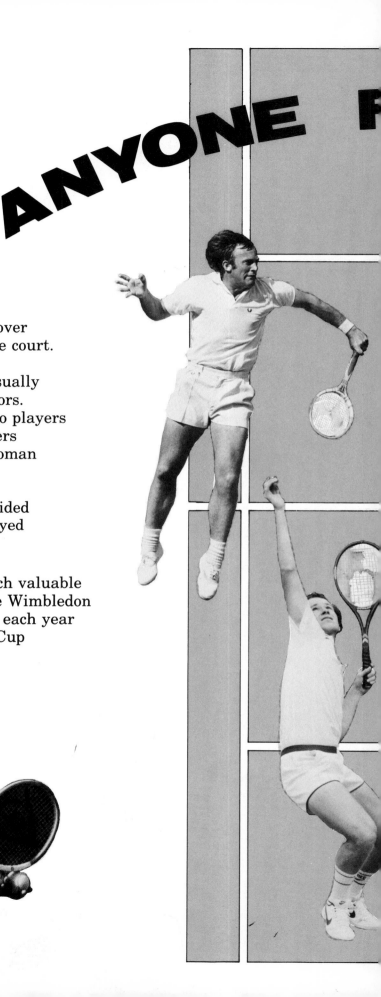

Tennis is a ball game. It is played with rackets
on a court. Players hit the ball back and forth over
a net. The net is strung across the middle of the court.

The game's proper name is lawn tennis. It is usually
thought of as a summer game, played out of doors.
Two or four people play together. A game of two players
is called a 'singles' match. A game of four players
is called a 'doubles' match. When a man and woman
team up, the match is called a 'mixed doubles'.

A tennis court is rectangular in shape. It is divided
into various playing areas. Tennis was first played
in England around 1873.

Each year, tennis tournaments are held at which valuable
prizes are given. The best known of these is the Wimbledon
Tournament. This tournament has been played each year
since 1877. The Davis Cup and the Whiteman Cup
are two other important competitions.

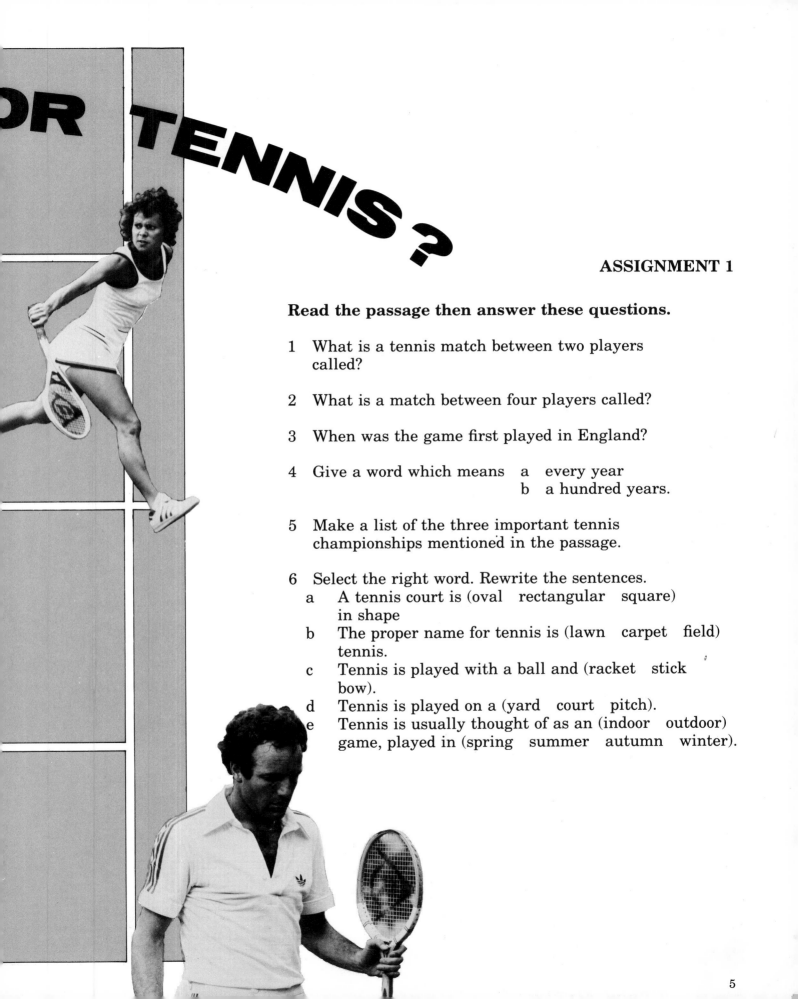

OR TENNIS?

Read the passage then answer these questions.

1   What is a tennis match between two players called?

2   What is a match between four players called?

3   When was the game first played in England?

4   Give a word which means   a   every year
                               b   a hundred years.

5   Make a list of the three important tennis championships mentioned in the passage.

6   Select the right word. Rewrite the sentences.
   a   A tennis court is (oval   rectangular   square) in shape
   b   The proper name for tennis is (lawn   carpet   field) tennis.
   c   Tennis is played with a ball and (racket   stick   bow).
   d   Tennis is played on a (yard   court   pitch).
   e   Tennis is usually thought of as an (indoor   outdoor) game, played in (spring   summer   autumn   winter).

5

WORD WORK 1   ASSIGNMENT 2

Match each of these words with its meaning.

ADEQUATE	a large tent	NASTY	to whiten
EXCLAIM	enough	GREEDY	equal in value
FINISH	a violent storm	BLEACH	a tune
HURRICANE	to wash and iron	EQUIVALENT	unpleasant
LAUNDER	to end	HOSTILE	wanting too much
MARQUEE	to cry out	MELODY	unfriendly

Write sentences. Use each of the words in a separate sentence.

WORD WORK 2   ASSIGNMENT 3

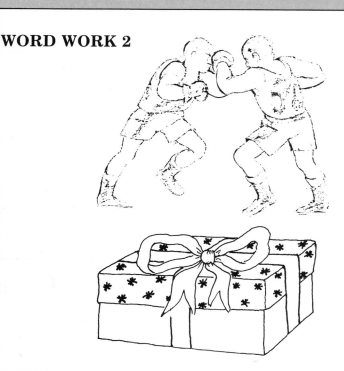

The word BOX is illustrated in the picture.

Box has two meanings
1. to fight, 2. a container

Here are some other words.
Each one has at least two different meanings.

date	watch	spring	bark
rose	stick	yard	think

Write sentences to show you understand the different meanings of each word.

WORD WORK 3   ASSIGNMENT 4

Write out the words in each line.
Underline the word in each line which is similar in meaning to the one in capitals.

ANSWER	shout	reply	whisper	talk
PLUCKY	strong	shy	brave	lucky
BRIGHT	show	flat	dull	shining
FALL	drop	raise	run	swim
REVEAL	have	hide	show	receive

LANGUAGE WORK 1   ASSIGNMENT 5

> Sentences begin with a capital letter.
> Sentences end with a full stop.

Write out this passage correctly.

CAMELS OF THE DESERT

camels are ugly animals yet they are very
useful they have been used by man for many
years camels are used in Africa and Asia
to carry goods across the desert there are
two kinds of camel the Asian camel has two
humps and a long shaggy coat the other kind
of camel is the African camel this one has a short
brown coat and only one hump a baby camel is
called a colt.

LANGUAGE WORK 2   ASSIGNMENT 6

Write suitable endings for these sentences.

1 Janet never likes ....

2 We are hoping...

3 Our school is ....

4 Every evening when...

5 People who live...

6 There is no room..

7 My favourite...

8 The police were called..

WRITING A LETTER – A REMINDER

Write out this letter correctly.

Seaview House Hotel, Burnham-on-Sea, Somerset.
20th July 1984. Dear Mum and Dad. I am having
a great time at Burnham. The weather has been hot
and I have gone down to the Royal Beach each day.
I will be coming home on Saturday. I will arrive
at Blackwood at six o'clock. Can you please meet
me at the bus station? Love, Sandra.

WRITING WORK 2 ASSIGNMENT 8

An aunt and uncle have written to you inviting you
to stay with them for a holiday at their home in
Bournemouth.

Write a letter of thanks saying you accept the invitation.
Tell them of your travel arrangements.

WRITING WORK 3 ASSIGNMENT 9

Each of these notices might be seen during a visit
to the countryside.

**Explain each of the notices and give a reason why you think
they were necessary.**

PUZZLE PAGE

THE A–Z PUZZLE (Part 1)

Ask your teacher for a copy of this puzzle.
Complete the puzzle by filling in the missing letters.

1   To do away with
2   Something bought cheaply
3   One hundredth birthday
4   The number below the line
    in a fraction
5   A violent shaking of the earth
6   Tiredness

7   Boat used on the canals of Venice
8   Shape with six equal sides
9   Regular part payment of a debt
10   A young person
11   Finger joints
12   An ocean-going passenger ship

#	1	2	3	4	5	6	7	8
1	A			L			H	
2	B		R			I		
3	C	E		T		A		
4	D		N		M		A		O
5	E	A			H		A		
6	F		T			U		
7	G			D			A	
8	H		X			O		
9	I			T			M	
10	J		V			I		
11	K	N			K			
12	L		N				

'THE BEST CAR IN THE WORLD'
ROLLS-ROYCE

This car is a Rolls-Royce. It is called a Silver Spirit.
Next to it you can see one of the first Rolls-Royces,
the first Silver Ghost. The first Silver Ghost was built in 1906.

Rolls and Royce are the names of the two men who began
the Rolls-Royce Motor Company.

Charles Rolls came from London. Henry Royce came from
Peterborough. After just one year their cars were hailed
'best in the world'. Eighty years later, the company they
began still has a high reputation.

Rolls-Royce are thought of as the makers of the world's
finest cars. Their cars also last the longest. Each
one is a superb piece of engineering. Half the cars
ever built by Rolls-Royce are still on the road.

Rolls-Royce take great care over their cars. Almost every
part of each car is individually made. Only highly
skilled craftsmen are allowed to work on the cars and only
the finest materials are used. Only twelve cars each day
are built by the company. Rolls-Royce cars are built
in Crewe.

Read the passage, then answer these questions.

1 Which two men set up a company in 1904 to build cars?

2 Which is true?: a They both came from London.
                  b They both came from Peterborough.
                  c They came from different places.

3 What were the Christian names of Rolls and Royce?

4 What was the name of the company founded by Rolls and Royce?

5 Which is true? A Silver Ghost is
                  a a haunting spirit
                  b a pop group
                  c a motor car

6 When was the first Silver Ghost built?

7 Rolls-Royce cars are thought of as the best in the world because
                  a they have pretty coloured paintwork
                  b they are well made
                  c more are made than any other kind of car
                  d they last a long time
                  e they are cheap

Which of these are correct?

8 How many cars are produced each day in their factory?

9 Where are Rolls-Royce cars made?

10 Find the word or words in the passage which mean
           a a dozen   c thought well of
           b able workmen   d one at a time

Choose the best meaning for each of the words listed below.

NOTE
a good mark
b short letter
c funny joke

COZY
a dark
b comfortable
c dirty

FROWN
a angry look
b pleased look
c happy look

HIKE
a small
b long walk
c nickname

WRENCH
a dish
b woman
c tool

FRET
a worry
b cry
c laugh

SNACK
a small meal
b low chair
c small house

ABILITY
a handicap
b skill
c hope

ORDINARY
a different
b strange
c commonplace

ARRIVE
a stay
b come
c go

FAKE
a loyal
b false
c healthy

LOCATE
a find
b lose
c choose

Write twelve sentences.
Use each of the words in capital letters in a separate sentence.

Arrange these words in dictionary order:

envoy   bagpipes   haven   jubilant
marquee   nimble   garbage   decay
arson   quest   throng   loiter
outcry   urge   cassock   vodka
impede   weasel   kale   radius
fissure   penetrate   scamper   xray
               yoga   zinc

Use your dictionary to find the meaning of the underlined words.
Write sentences. Use each word in a separate sentence.

LANGUAGE WORK 1

Write out these sentences.
Choose the correct word from the two in brackets and complete the sentences.

1 Mice (likes   like) cheese.
2 The soldiers (marches   march) down the road.
3 The pupils (was   were) out to play.
4 Betty (runs   run) in the race.
5 I went (swim   swimming) in the river.
6 My feet (is   are) hurting.
7 He (sing   sang) a lovely song.
8 Nigel and Sara (is   are) coming to my party.
9 Winston (come   came) to Birmingham
   from the West Indies.
10 Badhadur (want   wants) to be a doctor.

LANGUAGE WORK 2

Read this sentence:
    The sun shines.
This is a statement sentence, it gives information.
The statement gives information about the sun.
It tells us the sun is shining.

Write statements about each of these.

1 London   2 Nelson

3 winter   4 your teacher

5 bananas   6 the weather today

7 food   8 my class

9 the Prime Minister

LANGUAGE WORK 3

Some sentences ask questions.
    Where do you live? What is the time?

**Write ten question sentences which you might ask
an American visitor to your class.**

| USING THE TELEPHONE |

The telephone was invented by Alexander Graham Bell.

It is probably the most often used means of sending messages.

Billions of messages pass along telephone wires each day.

Here are a few simple hints on how to use the telephone.

1   Look up the number you want to call.
2   Look up the area code you need.
3   Pick up the receiver and wait for the 'dialling tone'. This is a continuous purring sound.
4   Dial slowly – first the area code followed by the number.
5   When the number answers, say who you are.

Write down the names and telephone numbers of the people in your class.
Arrange the names in dictionary order.

WRITING WORK 2   **ASSIGNMENT 18**

In almost every part of Britain, dialling 999 will connect you with the EMERGENCY SERVICES.

These are the six main emergency services:

FIRE   POLICE   AMBULANCE

COASTGUARD   CAVE RESCUE   MOUNTAIN RESCUE

Find a telephone directory.

Find out what information you will be asked for when you dial 999.

WRITING WORK 3   **ASSIGNMENT 19**

Maybe you have already had to dial 999.

Write an account of the circumstances which caused you to do so.

PUZZLE PAGE

ASSIGNMENT 20

Ask your teacher for a copy of this puzzle.
Fit each of these words into the puzzle.
Fit the words so that the last two letters
of each word become the first two letters of the next.

ABROAD	ADJECTIVE	ALLURE	ANTAGONIST
APPEAR	APPETITE	ARSONIST	CHARGE
DEFINE	EDITOR	ELOPE	ENCORE
ERASE	GEOGRAPHY	HYDROGEN	LEAP
LEISURE	NEITHER	ORANGES	PERCH
REAP	RELISH	RELIVE	REPTILE
SENSIBLE	SHORE	STAMPEDE	STARTED
TEETOTAL	VESSEL	VETERAN	

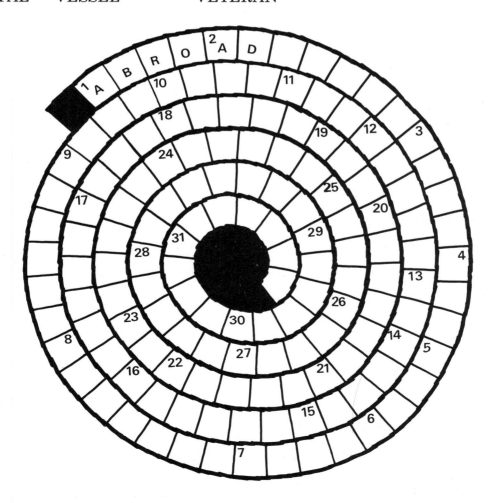

The River Horse of Africa

The hippo (full name hippopotamus) is a big animal.
Its name means 'river horse'. Its home is in the rivers
and lakes of the hot African forests.
The hippo likes to sunbathe.

A fully-grown hippo may weigh up to four tons.
The animal has a big body, gaping mouth and short,
stubby legs. When they walk, hippos appear to be slow.
But they can move quickly if they are frightened or angry.

The animal has two shiny eyes. These are high up
on its head, so the hippo can see all around him.

Hippos like each other's company. In the forest, they
are often found in herds, playing together. During the
day, hippos rest and sleep. When the cool evening
comes, they get up and begin to search for food.
The hippo eats mostly soft, green, tender leaves
and branches.

The hippo has few enemies. Very young hippos
are sometimes killed by crocodiles.

Read the passage, then answer the questions.

1   What is the full name of a hippo?

2   A river horse is a: a   a horse who likes to swim
                                       b   a hippopotamus
                                       c   a clothes horse

3   A fully grown hippo will weigh about:
                                       a   4 tons
                                       b   2 tons 5lbs
                                       c   6 tons 4oz

4   Which adjectives describe the hippo's legs?

5   During the day hippos like to:
                                       a   search for food
                                       b   swim in the river
                                       c   rest and sleep

6   Hippos are found in:
                                       a   Scotland
                                       b   Russia
                                       c   Africa

7   What does the hippo feed on?

8   When will a hippo move quickly?

9   Find the word in the passage which means:
                                       a   thick woods
                                       b   an open, stretching mouth
                                       c   a group of animals

10   High is the opposite of low. Find the word
    in the passage which is opposite to:
                                       a   cold
                                       b   dull
                                       c   hard

WORD WORK 1

Find one word for each of these phrases.
The first one has been done for you.

1 to go by air (fly)
2 to go back (re . . . .)
3 to go down (de . . . . .)
4 to go with (ac . . . .)
5 to go up (as . . . .)
6 to go into (en . . .)
7 to chase (pu . . . .)
8 to walk in step (m . . . .)
9 to go by boat (s . . .)
10 to go and live abroad (em . . . . . .)

WORD WORK 2

Each word in set 1 is connected with a word in set 2.
For example: actress is connected with theatre.
Find pairs of words and write them in your book.

Set 1

theatre	moat	car	television	church	horse
tree	café	boxer	hedgerow	seaside	aeroplane
knight	kitchen	dairy	chicken		

Set 2

castle	armour	saddle	screen	licence
food	eggs	gloves	altar	sink
hangar	leaves	beach	cows	actress
wild flowers				

WORD WORK 3

Write out these pairs of words.
If they are similar in meaning write S after them.
If they are opposite in meaning write O.

1 shout whisper
2 stay remain
3 found lost
4 first last
5 close near
6 ascend descend
7 separate unite
8 careful cautious
9 front back
10 impure pure
11 clean dirty
12 rich poor
13 fear terror
14 bleak dreary
15 hold release
16 colossal gigantic

| PUNCTUATION — USING THE COMMA |

RULE 1
You use commas to separate items in a list.
   For example: In the car he carried a first-aid kit,
                  a fire extinguisher, tool box, torch
                  and pump.

RULE 2
You use commas in a sentence to separate
a list of actions.
   For example: I dug a trench, planted the seeds, watered
                  the ground and filled in the trench.
Notice that you do not put a comma before or after
the word 'and'.

RULE 3
You use commas to separate phrases beginning
with the words when, if, although and because.
   For example: When you have finished, you can go home.

Punctuate these sentences.
1   I saw potatoes cabbages carrots and onions
    on the market stall.
2   Crocuses daffodils iris and primulas all bloom
    in Spring.
3   Oranges lemons limes pineapples and mangoes
    do not grow in Britain.
4   The spectators left the match because it began to rain.
5   When you come in from the garden take your shoes off.
6   Although it looked like rain the match began on time.

Poetry page

There are several poems about the hippopotamus.
Here is one fun poem about it.

THE HABITS OF THE HIPPOPOTAMUS

The hippopotamus is strong
   And huge of head and broad of bustle;
The limbs on which he rolls along
   Are big with hippopotomuscle.

He does not greatly care for sweets
   Like ice cream, apple pie, or custard,
But takes to flavour what he eats
   A little hippopotomustard.

The hippopotamus is true
   To all his principles, and just;
He always tries his best to do
   The things one hippopotomust.

He never rides in trucks or trams,
   In taxicabs or omnibuses,
And so keeps out of traffic jams
   And other hippotomusses.

Arthur Guiterman

---

1   Read the poem and, if you wish, copy it into your book.

2   Explain: a   broad of bustle
             b   true to all his principles

3   What does the hippo use to flavour his food?

4   What are omnibuses?

5   Hippopotomuscle is a nonsense word.
    What other nonsense words are in the poem?

6   In the last two lines of the poem, the poet
    suggests that the hippo keeps out of the way of other hippos.

    Is this true? Read page 14 again.

PUZZLE PAGE

WORD DOMINOES

Ask your teacher for a copy of this puzzle.

Fit the words below into the puzzle.
Write each six letter word in a clockwise direction,
starting in the numbered square.

Wherever dominoes meet, the letters in the adjoining squares match each other.
The first word, radial, has been put in for you.

ABROAD	ADVERT	AROUND	CAMERA	RODENT	PREFER
CINEMA	DESIGN	EFFORT	HIDDEN	SENSES	POETIC
HORROR	ISLAND	MONKEY	MUSEUM	STAYED	REDDEN
MUSTER	NUMBER	ORANGE	PRAYER	YACHTS	READER

RUGBY
The Welsh Obsession

Every Welsh village has a rugby team. There are few Welshmen who have not played the game.
Rugby is the national sport of Wales. For many Welsh people the game is an obsession.

Three or four times during the rugby season, Welsh villages become almost deserted. The people all go to Cardiff. There at the famous Arms Park they take part in a festival of rugby – an international match.

At the international, the Welsh team pit their strength and skill against the visitors. Teams from England, Scotland, Ireland and France come to Cardiff. Sometimes the visitors are the famous 'All Blacks'. The 'All Blacks' come from New Zealand. Their visit always causes great excitement.

Rugby began at Rugby school. A game like soccer had been played there for many years. In 1823 during one of these games, a player picked up the ball and ran with it. This was the beginning of rugby. The player's name was William Webb-Ellis. He is now thought of as the 'Father of the Game'.

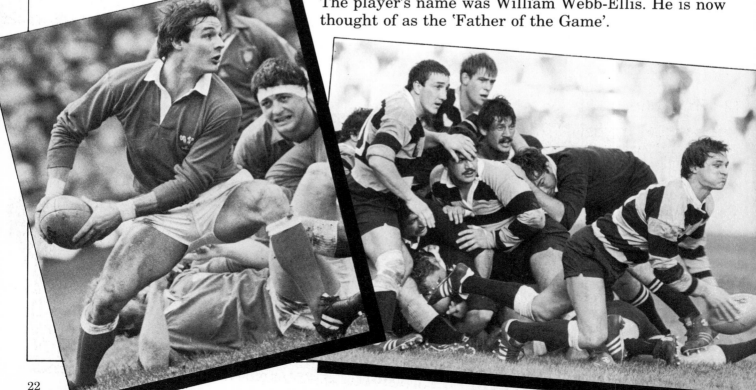

Read the passage, then answer these questions.

1   What is the national sport of Wales?

2   Use your dictionary to find the meaning of:
      a   obsession
      b   deserted
      c   international

3   Which countries take part regularly in the rugby international series?

4   Who are the 'All Blacks'?
    Which country do they come from?

5   In the passage one important difference between soccer and rugby is mentioned.
      What is this difference?
      Can you name another?

6   At which school did rugby football begin?

7   How did the game begin?
    How long ago was this?

8   Who is regarded as the 'Father of Rugby Football'?

9   What is the name of Cardiff's famous rugby field?
    Is it: a   Landsdown Park
             b   The Vetch
             c   The Dell
             d   The Arms Park

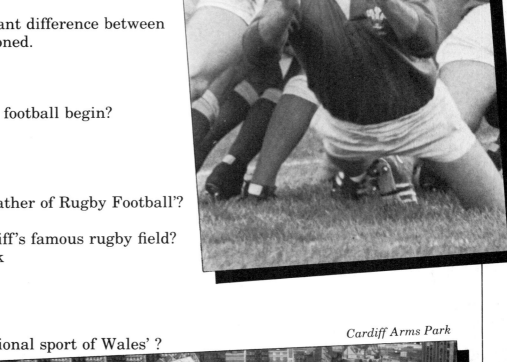

Cardiff Arms Park

10   What is meant by 'the national sport of Wales'?

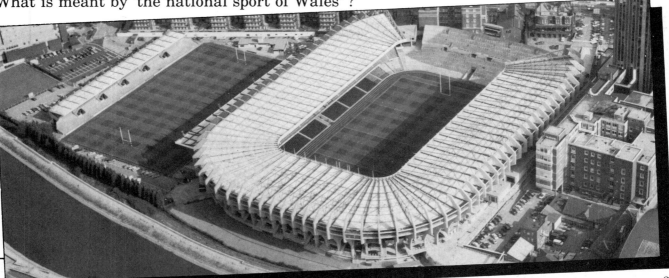

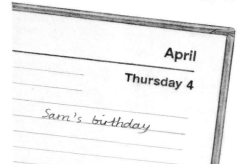

April   dawn   grubby   explained
choir   earthquake become   disqualified

**Change the words underlined in each sentence
for one of the words above.**

1   They got up early to see <u>the coming of daylight</u>.
2   All of a sudden there was a <u>great shaking</u>
    <u>of the earth's surface</u>.
3   My birthday falls during <u>the fourth month of the year</u>.
4   Janet has <u>grown to be</u> a beautiful lady.
5   We could hear a <u>group of singers</u> performing
    in the church.
6   The referee <u>put out of the game</u> the centre forward.
7   The teacher <u>made clear</u> the meaning of the chapter.
8   The children looked very <u>dirty and untidy</u>.

Some words have two different spellings
and meanings, although they sound alike.

**Write sentences to show you understand the meaning
of each of these words.**

beech beach   hale hail   key quay
where wear   sale sail   fête fate

MORE PRACTICE WITH COMMAS

Copy, correct and punctuate these sentences.

1 sparrows finches thrushes and blackbirds live
   in the wood
2 in the gym there were wallbars a jumping horse
   mats and ropes
3 although she was feeling ill she still continued
   with the game
4 i filled the kettle waited for it to boil
   put the tea in the pot and poured on the water
5 if the snow thaws you will not be able
   to go skiing
6 because of the storm the ship was unable to dock
7 we went into the field picked some strawberries
   took them home put sugar and cream on them
   and had them for tea
8 if you come to the party please wear a tie

Here are ten groups of words.
Write ten sentences.
Use a different group of words in each sentence.

1 Thames Wye Severn Avon
2 Dorset Surrey Northumberland Gwent
3 Asia Europe Africa
4 Geography History Maths and English
5 dark damp gloomy
6 small frisky black and white
7 knives forks spoons and plates
8 soft brown furry
9 cold wet cloudy
10 green yellow brown and gold

Rugby and soccer are the two most important ball games played in Britain.
Every week, during the season, hundreds take part in these sports and thousands watch.

Write about the games.

How many players are in   a   a soccer team
                           b   a rugby team?

Make a list of the 'positions' for each game.
Draw plans of a rugby pitch and a soccer pitch.
Mark on your plans the positions of the players at the beginning of a game.

Do you support a particular team?
If you are a team supporter write all you can about this season's matches.
Make a list, in alphabetical order, of the names of the players.
Make a list of the team's fixtures.
Does your team have a supporters' club?
If there is a club, make a list of the membership rules.

Sports Reporter
Go and watch the next school home match.
Write a description of the game.
Record who scores.
Record any special movements.
Record the names of the captain and players.

PUZZLE PAGE

Ask your teacher for a copy of this puzzle.
Complete the puzzle.

Here are some clues to help you.

Clues across

1 Second month
5 Opposite of subtract
7 Arms and legs
9 To obtain
10 To encounter
12 Past tense of dream
15 Source of light
16 Young cow
18 A portion
20 Turns the lock
21 Done without difficulty
22 Opposite of near

Clues down

1 Past tense of fight
2 Floats on water
3 Not pretty
4 To recall
6 To make up ones mind
8 Produced by boiling water
11 Noah took two of each into the Ark
13 To hunt down
14 Not young
17 To move through the air
19 Used in road surfacing

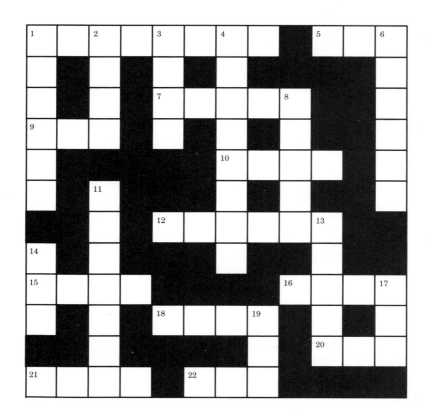

Mountaineering

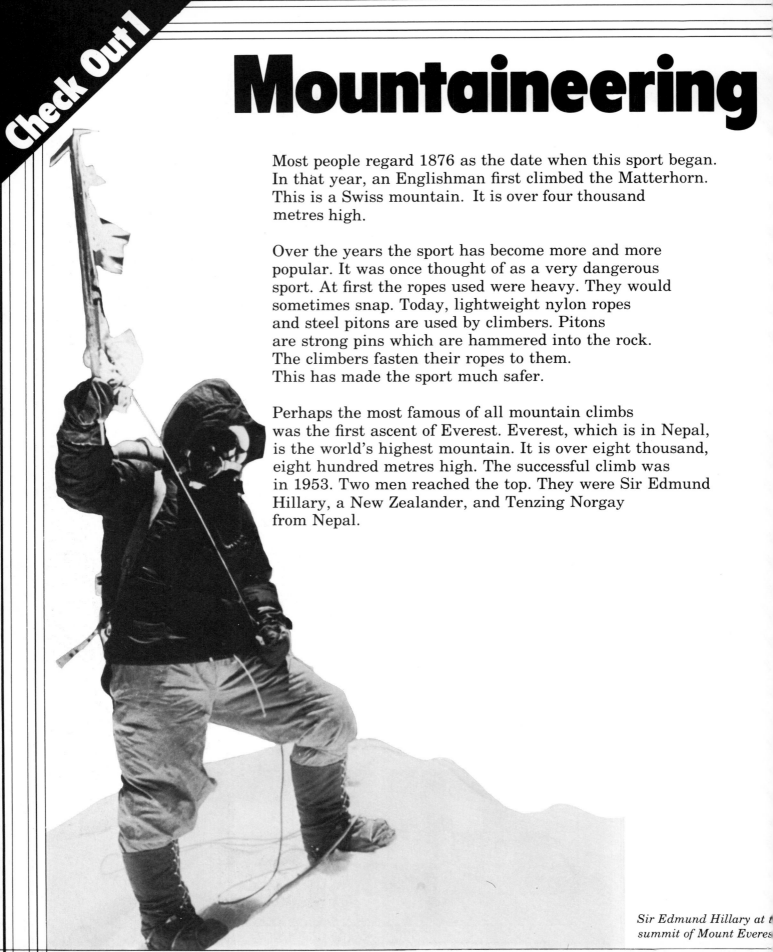

Most people regard 1876 as the date when this sport began. In that year, an Englishman first climbed the Matterhorn. This is a Swiss mountain. It is over four thousand metres high.

Over the years the sport has become more and more popular. It was once thought of as a very dangerous sport. At first the ropes used were heavy. They would sometimes snap. Today, lightweight nylon ropes and steel pitons are used by climbers. Pitons are strong pins which are hammered into the rock. The climbers fasten their ropes to them. This has made the sport much safer.

Perhaps the most famous of all mountain climbs was the first ascent of Everest. Everest, which is in Nepal, is the world's highest mountain. It is over eight thousand, eight hundred metres high. The successful climb was in 1953. Two men reached the top. They were Sir Edmund Hillary, a New Zealander, and Tenzing Norgay from Nepal.

Sir Edmund Hillary at the summit of Mount Everest

Read the passage, then answer these questions.

1 What is the sport of mountain climbing called?

2 When did the sport begin?

3 Is the world's highest mountain:
    a Mount Everest
    b Snowdon
    c The Matterhorn?

5 Is the world's highest mountain in:
    a Scotland
    b Switzerland
    c Nepal?

6 Who were the first climbers to reach
  the top of Mount Everest?

7 When did they successfully climb Mount Everest?

8 What are pitons?
  Which three adjectives describe them?

9 The Matterhorn is in Switzerland.
  It is described as a Swiss mountain.
  How would you describe a mountain in:
    a France   c Wales
    b Scotland   d Ireland?

Equipment used by mountaineers

10 Which word or words in the passage mean:
    a best known
    b liked by an increasing number of people
    c not safe?

11 What is the difference between the height
  of the Matterhorn and of Mount Everest?

WORD WORK 1

Take the correct word from the brackets to complete these sentences.

1 His brother . . . . where he had been.(guest, guessed)
2 There is an interesting . . . . on TV. (serial, cereal)
3 The Queen gave her . . . . to the new law. (ascent, assent)
4 The car was . . . . at the time of the accident. (stationery, stationary)
5 Queen Victoria had a long . . . . (reign, rain)

WORD WORK 2

Match each word with its meaning.

ADEQUATE	wanting too much	EQUIVALENT	a skill
MARQUEE	enough	LOCATE	to whiten
HOSTILE	a large tent	BLEACH	equal in value
ORDINARY	unfriendly	ABILITY	to look displeased
GREEDY	commonplace	FROWN	to find

WORD WORK 3

**Copy the list of words printed in capital letters.
By the side of each write the word which is similar in meaning.**

1	COLLECT	sweep	gather	clean	jump
2	SHORT	dark	tall	brief	long
3	HIDE	seek	ask	show	conceal
4	SHOW	act	reveal	draw	dance
5	TOP	summit	vase	middle	bottom

WORD WORK 4

**Copy the list of words printed in capital letters.
By the side of each write the word which is opposite in meaning.**

1	NOISE	shout	row	quiet	scream
2	CLEAN	bathed	dirty	washed	ill
3	HOT	cold	warm	sun	fire
4	DAY	afternoon	dawn	night	morning
5	SHALLOW	small	thin	deep	paddle

LANGUAGE WORK 1

Copy and punctuate these sentences.

1 I went into my classroom sat at my desk got out my books and began writing

2 My grocer sells fresh bacon eggs butter milk vegetables and cheese

3 I will cook dinner when my brother comes home

4 Although it began to rain we still went down to the beach

5 I missed my interview because the train was late

6 We will all go on holiday if we pass our exams

LANGUAGE WORK 2

Using each of these words or phrases once, write 8 different statement sentences.

1 pans
2 Drake
3 your headteacher
4 summer
5 oranges
6 yesterday's weather
7 breakfast
8 your friend

LANGUAGE WORK 3

These sentences are all statement sentences.
Turn them into question sentences.
The first one has been done for you.

1 It is raining. Is it raining?
2 I heard the cuckoo this morning.
3 I had an egg for my breakfast.
4 There are one hundred pence in a pound.
5 'The Dam Busters' is an interesting book.
6 We went to Benidorm for our holidays.
7 Your hair is turning grey.
8 You felt pain in your legs.

WRITING WORK 1

Here are six notices which we see from time
to time.

Write three sentences about each one.
Suggest where you might see the notice.
Who would put up such a notice?
Why do you think the notice is necessary?

WRITING WORK 2

Pretend you have a friend named Tim Evans.
Your friend lives at 26 Corporation Road, Newcastle-upon-Tyne.

**Write a letter to your friend inviting him to spend
a weekend with you.**
Write about your home. Say whom your friend will meet.
What will you do together?
Mention what arrangements you will make to meet him.

WRITING WORK 3

VANDALS CAUSE BABY'S DEATH
Write the story behind this news item.

Poetry page

THE COW

The friendly cow all red and white
I love with all my heart,
She gives me cream with all her might
To eat with apple-tart.

She wanders lowing here and there,
And yet she cannot stray,
All in the pleasant open air,
The pleasant light of day.

And blown by all the winds that pass,
And wet with all the showers,
She walks amid the meadow grass,
And eats the meadow flowers.

R L Stevenson

**Read the poem,
then answer the questions.**

1 Jersey cows are light brown.
   Hereford cows are red and white.
   Fresians are black and white.
   Which breed of cow is the one in the poem?

2 Why does the poet like the cow so much?

3 Which word describes the sound cows make?

4 Write down two phrases which suggest unpleasant
   weather.

5 Explain in a few words these phrases:
   a   with all her might
   b   she cannot stray
   c   amid the meadow grass

WINSTON CHURCHILL

Many people think of Winston Churchill as Britain's greatest leader. He is remembered as the man who led Britain to victory in the Second World War (1939–45).

Churchill was born in 1874. His birthplace was Blenheim Palace, in Oxfordshire.

As a young man, Churchill became a soldier. He fought in South Africa and was captured by the enemy. When the First World War came (1914–18), Churchill was put in command of the navy.

In 1939, war came again to Britain. We call this the Second World War. Churchill soon became Prime Minister. As leader, he told the British people that the road to victory would be hard. He told them, 'I offer you nothing but blood, toil, tears and sweat.' Through the war years, Churchill's speeches inspired the people.

Everywhere he went crowds cheered him. They recognized him by the big, fat cigar which he always seemed to be smoking. Churchill always waved back with his V for Victory sign.

Churchill died in 1965 and was buried in Bladon churchyard near his birthplace.

The North Portico of Blenheim Palace

Churchill a prisoner of the Boers (right)

Read the passage, then answer these questions.

1 When and where was Churchill born?

2 Is Blenheim Palace near:
    a Oxford
    b Cardiff
    c Edinburgh

3 When he was a young man, Churchill became:
    a a doctor
    b a student
    c a soldier

4 Churchill led the people of Britain during the:
    a Wars of the Roses
    b Napoleonic wars
    c Second World War

5 When did the Second World War begin?

6 When did the war end?

7 During wartime, how was Churchill often recognized?

8 When did Churchill die and where was he buried?

9 How old was Churchill:
    a at the beginning of the First World War
    b at the end of the Second World War
    c when he died

10 Which word or words in the passage mean the same as
    a in charge
    b hard work
    c many people

NAMING WORDS: NOUNS

A noun is a naming word.
A noun is the name of a person, animal,
place or thing.

Copy these sentences into your book.
Underline the nouns in each sentence.

1   The farmer took the horses into the field near the river.

2   The car was driven by a woman wearing a jumper,
    skirt and dark glasses.

3   Lions, tigers, bears and monkeys can be seen
    in the zoo.

4   David, Jean, Brian and Julie are all going
    to the disco at the Youth Club.

5   Knives, forks, spoons, cups, saucers and plates
    all had to be put in boxes ready for camp.

6   We went to the farm and picked strawberries,
    raspberries, peas, beans and potatoes.

7   There were two bars, a restaurant, three shops,
    a room to play games, a lounge and a pool on board
    the liner.

8   The plane landed, taxied along the runway
    and stopped near the terminal.

LANGUAGE WORK 2   **ASSIGNMENT 39**

The words in the list below can be divided
into five groups: insects, fruits, flowers, birds
and fish.
Write them out in their five groups.

wasp	mosquito	hake	trout	robin
cod	rose	blackbird	iris	apple
ant	salmon	daisy	eagle	fly
sole	ladybird	hawk	buttercup	lemon
daffodil	sparrow	pear	plum	orange

PROPER NOUNS

Read these sentences.

I live in Meadowbank Road.
I go to Blackwood School.
My friend is Kang Chang.

Meadowbank Road, Blackwood School, Kang Chang
are proper nouns.
A proper noun is the name of a particular person,
place or thing.
Proper nouns always begin with capital letters.

Write down the names of five

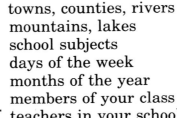
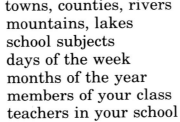

towns, counties, rivers
mountains, lakes
school subjects
days of the week
months of the year
members of your class
teachers in your school

LANGUAGE WORK 4   **ASSIGNMENT 41**

In this list, ten of the names are proper nouns.
They should begin with a capital letter.
Decide which are the proper nouns. Write them in your book.
Write ten sentences.

Use a different proper noun in each sentence.

thursday	girl	boy	july	dog
easter	sheep	cow	birmingham	history
orange	david	book	factory	woolworths
diamonds	jewels	goliath	parliament	wales

AIR SEA RESCUE

The beginning of this story is written for you.
The picture will also help you with your writing.
Copy the story into your book and finish it.

David and Andrew Thomas were on holiday at the seaside.
On the second day of their holiday, they decided to walk
along the beach to Rest Bay. It was about half a mile.
The two boys set off. They explored some
rock pools. They did not notice the tide had raced
in and they were cut off ...

Here are some words and phrases which may help you
with your writing.

climb the cliffs	panic	telephone	harness
thundering waves	coast guard	helicopter	submerged
shouting for help	binoculars	winched up	ordeal

PUZZLE PAGE

ANAGRAMS

Ask your teacher for a copy of this puzzle.
Look at the word MEAT. The same letters make the word MATE.
MATE is an anagram of MEAT.

Copy and complete the puzzle by writing anagrams for each of the words.

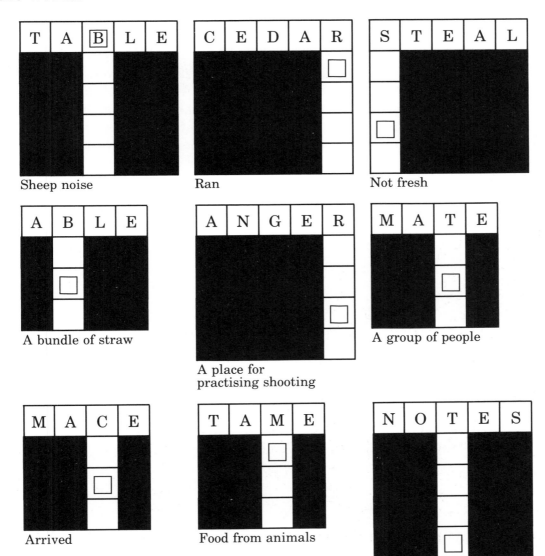

T	A	B	L	E	

Sheep noise

C	E	D	A	R

Ran

S	T	E	A	L

Not fresh

A	B	L	E

A bundle of straw

A	N	G	E	R

A place for practising shooting

M	A	T	E

A group of people

M	A	C	E

Arrived

T	A	M	E

Food from animals

N	O	T	E	S

Sounds

If your anagrams are correct, the letters
in each box will make two words.

Answer: – – –   – – – – –

The Lake District

Some people think the Lake District is the most beautiful part of Britain. The Lake District is an area in the north-west of England. It is a land of lakes and rugged mountains.

The Lake District is a holiday centre. In the district people can go fishing, sailing, swimming, walking, camping and climbing.

Most of the Lake District lies within the county of Cumbria. Almost the whole district is rural and covers an area of 2000 square kilometres. There are fifteen lakes within the area. The best-known of these is Lake Windermere. This is the largest lake in England. It is a narrow lake with many small islands.

England's highest mountain is in the Lake District. It is called Scafell Pike. It is 978 metres high.

Some of Britain's greatest poets have lived around the lakes. Among them were Wordsworth and Coleridge. With their friends they became famous as 'the Lake Poets'. Many of their poems are about the lakes, the mountains and the things they saw while walking in this beautiful part of Britain.

Read the passage, then answer the questions.

1 Where in England is the Lake District?

2 What is the area of the Lake District?

3 What sporting activities take place in the district?

4 Which is England's highest mountain?
   a Matterhorn
   b Snowdon
   c Scafell Pike

5 How high is this mountain?

6 What is the name of England's largest lake?

7 How many lakes are there in the Lake District?
   a five
   b fifteen
   c twenty-five

8 Name two of the Lake Poets.

9 Coleridge is a proper noun.
   Find five other proper nouns
   in the passage.

10 Which word or words in the passage mean:
    a thin
    b a country area
    c people who write poetry
    d England, Scotland and Wales

Poetry page

The Lake District, with its vast stretches of water, high mountains, wooded hills, rushing streams and small hillside sheep farms, has inspired many poets.

Three of the most famous were William and his sister Dorothy Wordsworth and another poet, Samuel Taylor Coleridge.

Perhaps the best known of all Lakeland poems is this one.

DAFFODILS

I wander'd lonely as a cloud
That floats on high o'er vales and hills,
When all at once I saw a crowd,
A host of golden daffodils;
Beside the lake, beneath the trees,
Fluttering and dancing in the breeze.

Continuous as the stars that shine
And twinkle on the Milky Way,
They stretched in never-ending line,
Along the margin of a bay:
Ten thousand saw I at a glance,
Tossing their heads in sprightly dance.

The waves beside them danced; but they
Out-did the sparkling waves in glee:
A poet could not be but gay,
In such a jocund company:
I gazed – and gazed – but little thought
What wealth the show to me had brought:

For oft, when on my couch I lie
In vacant or in pensive mood,
They flash upon that inward eye
Which is the bliss of solitude;
And then my heart with pleasure fills,
And dances with the daffodils.

William Wordsworth

Copy the poem into your book.

Draw and colour a picture of the scene the poet saw 'beside the lake, beneath the trees'.

William Wordsworth

Dorothy Wordsworth

Samuel Taylor Coleridge

1 Was the poet: a in a hurry
               b strolling quietly
               c marching along

2 Did he see on his walk: a some golden daffodils
                         b some angels
                         c a flock of sheep

3 Is the Milky Way: a the road to a cowshed
                  b a chocolate bar
                  c a collection of stars

4 Which words in the poem mean: a thoughtful
                              b happy
                              c a settee

5 a In verse 1 which word rhymes with trees?
   b In verse 2 which word rhymes with shine?
   c In verse 3 which word rhymes with thought?
   d In verse 4 which word rhymes with lie?

6 The poem is called 'Daffodils'.
   Can you suggest another title for the poem?

7 The words 'above' and 'behind' tell us the position of things.
   Find four other positional words in the poem.

8 The word golden is an adjective.
   It describes (tells us more) about the daffodils.
   Which adjectives describe: a dance
                                b waves
                                c company

WORD WORK 1 ASSIGNMENT 47

Choose the correct word from inside the brackets.

1 Does one (eat   keep   pay) a compliment?
2 A hoe is used for (digging   cutting   loosening) the soil.
3 Does one (pay   want   try) a penalty?
4 A martinet is a very (lazy   strict   silly) person.
5 Is a felon a (criminal   bird   fish)?
6 If you are constrained, are you (prevented   embarrassed   unwell)?
7 Does a meteorologist study (bones   weather   rocks)?
8 Does an obituary tell of a (birth   marriage   death)?

WORD WORK 2 ASSIGNMENT 48

Find a general name for each of the following groups.

1 sole plaice haddock cod . . . .fish. . . .

2 ants bees wasps beetles . . . .

3 chair table settee stool . . . .

4 knives spoons forks . . . .

5 lizard crocodile snake . . . .

6 salt pepper mustard . . . .

7 iron tin lead . . . .

8 bronze brass gun-metal . . . .

9 water cola vinegar . . . .

10 oxygen hydrogen nitrogen . . . .

WORD WORK 3 ASSIGNMENT 49

Look up the meanings of these words.
Write the meaning of each one in your notebook.
Use each word in a separate sentence.

supervise   superior   superintendent
intercept   interfere   international

PUZZLE PAGE

Ask your teacher for a copy of this puzzle.

Complete the word puzzle first.
This will help you decode the long puzzle at the bottom of the page.

1 Opposite of left
2 Unwanted plant
3 Small flat European country
4 Reptile – cold blooded animal
5 To be the same as – used in maths
6 To be away
7 Eaten on Shrove Tuesday
8 Comes after four and before six

	A	B	C	D	E	F	G	H
1	■	■						■
2					■	■	■	
3	■							
4					■	■		
5	■						■	
6							■	
7								
8	■	■	■					■

Decode rows:

| 2A | 1F | 3C | | 2A | 1C | 3C | 1G | 2B | | 1G | 1C | 2C | 3F | 4A | 5D | 1C | 4E |

| 1D | 4A | 3E | 5E | 4B | 3H | | | 1G | 3B | 5B | | 6B | 3C | 3C | 4D | |

| 6A | 6B | 3C | 5D | 1G | | 7A | 1D | 1C | 7B | 1G | 2B | 7H | | 4C | 7C | 3H | |

| 1G | 3B | 6D | 1D | 1C | | 4A | 2B | 7B | 1C | 7D | 3B | | 8D | 3C | 1C | |

| 1F | 1D | 2D | 3H | 7G | 3G | | 6F | 1C | 5B | 7B | 4A | 5D | 1C | 7G | | ? |

| 4C | 4B | 7H | 2A | 2C | 1C |

| 1C | 3C | 6B | 6D | 1C | 6F | | 3E | 3C | 5D | 1D | 6C | | 6C | 1G | 4E | 8F | 7G | 7C | 7H | 3C | 3G |

Cutty Sark

Cutty Sark is a famous sailing ship. She can be seen near the Thames at Greenwich, London. The ship is called a clipper. Clippers were very fast sailing ships.

Cutty Sark had three thousand square metres of sail. In full sail and with a strong wind the ships could reach a speed of seventeen knots. The first clippers were built around 1800. They got their name because of their high speeds. Their fast speeds made it possible for them to 'clip off' or shorten the time taken to complete a long voyage.

Cutty Sark was built in 1869. The ship is sixty-five metres long and twelve metres wide. Cutty Sark was first used to bring tea from China. After that she carried wool from Australia. For a time the ship was owned by a Portuguese merchant. He named her the 'Fereira'. However, after twenty-seven years she was sold again to a British merchant who gave her back her name, Cutty Sark.

Read the passage then answer these questions.

1   What type of ship is the Cutty Sark?
    a   a steamship
    b   nuclear submarine
    c   a clipper

2   Where can she be seen?

3   When were the first clippers built?

4   They were given this name because:
    a   they shortened the time needed
        for a long voyage
    b   they bumped into other ships
        and damaged them
    c   they were pirate boats

5   What speed could they sail at?

6   What did Cutty Sark do?
    a   carry coal to Newcastle
    b   carry tea from China
    c   catch whales

7   Who gave the ship the name 'Fereira'?

8   How long and how wide is the Cutty Sark?

9   People from Portugal are called Portuguese.
    Give the names of people from:
    a   Australia
    b   China
    c   Britain

10 In which year was the Cutty Sark sold
    to the British merchant?

Four-masted Barque

Trading Brigantine

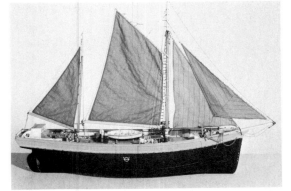

Trading Ketch

American Schooner

WORD WORK 1

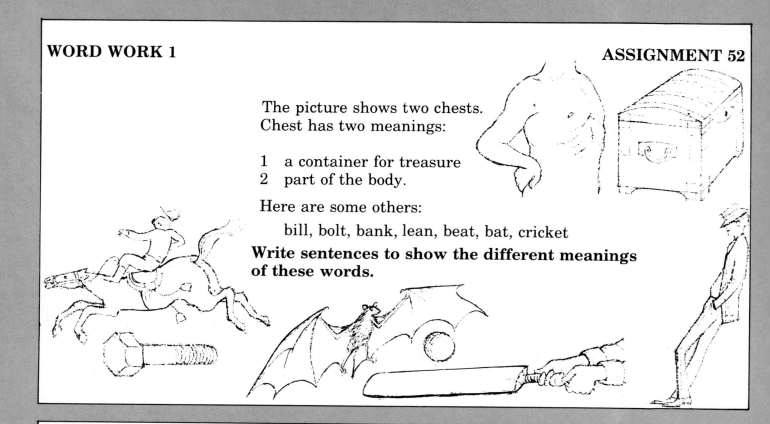

The picture shows two chests.
Chest has two meanings:

1　a container for treasure
2　part of the body.

Here are some others:

bill, bolt, bank, lean, beat, bat, cricket

**Write sentences to show the different meanings
of these words.**

WORD WORK 2

Match each of these words with its meaning.

POSTPONE	a graceful dance
MINUET	a thick, sweet liquid
SYRUP	a large stone
ANCIENT	to hate
BOULDER	shy and modest
FIGHT	not to remember
FORGET	very old
DAINTY	to put off until later
DETEST	a struggle or combat
CHIDE	to scold somebody
BASHFUL	delicate, pretty

**Write sentences to show
you understand the meaning
of each of the words.**

$\boxed{\text{COLLECTIVE NOUNS}}$

Words that stand for a group of people, animals
or things are called COLLECTIVE NOUNS.
For example: A <u>flock</u> of sheep, a <u>crowd</u> of people.

Write six other collective nouns in your book.

LANGUAGE WORK 2   **ASSIGNMENT 55**

school	flight	library
anthology	squad	bunch
choir	fleet	bouquet
orchestra	team	troupe

**Copy these phrases into your book.
Write at the side of each phrase
the most suitable collective noun
taken from those in the box.**

For example, a number of people – crowd.

A number of . . .

ships	whales	soldiers
poems	musicians	books
singers	dancers	cut flowers
steps	grapes	sports people

LANGUAGE WORK 3   **ASSIGNMENT 56**

**Substitute one of these for the word or words
underlined in each of the sentences below.**

a litter of	a suite	a swarm of
a flight of	fleet	a herd of
a school of	an anthology	

1 The cat had <u>several</u> kittens.
2 <u>Many</u> bees were found in the orchard.
3 <u>Many</u> steps led up to the flat.
4 Traffic stopped when <u>some</u> cows strayed into the road.
5 My parents bought a new <u>settee and arm chairs</u>
   for the lounge.
6 The <u>fishing boats</u> left the harbour early in the morning.
7 <u>Several</u> large whales were sighted near the headland.
8 The book contained <u>lots</u> of poems.

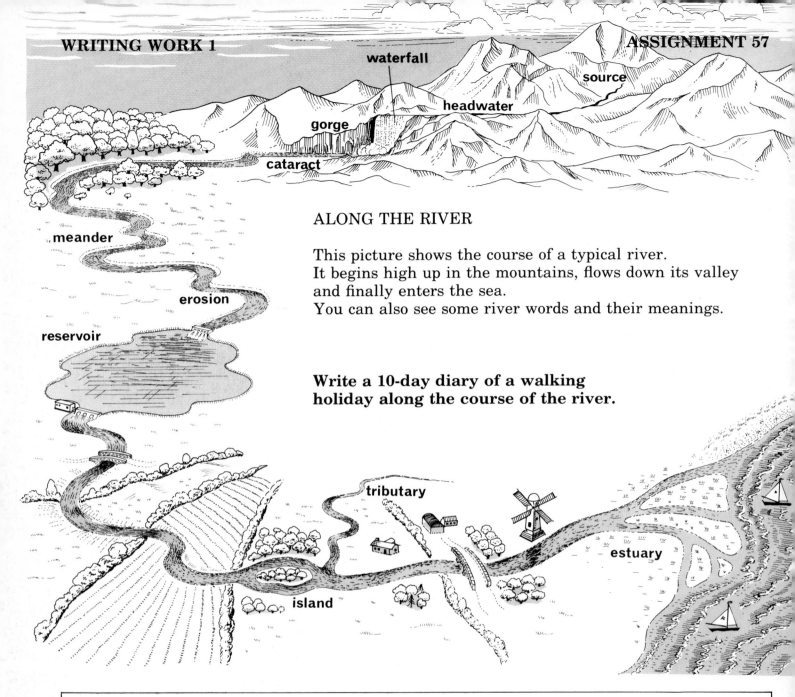

ALONG THE RIVER

This picture shows the course of a typical river.
It begins high up in the mountains, flows down its valley
and finally enters the sea.
You can also see some river words and their meanings.

**Write a 10-day diary of a walking
holiday along the course of the river.**

WRITING WORK 2   **ASSIGNMENT 58**

Write an adventure story with a riverside setting.

WRITING WORK 3   **ASSIGNMENT 59**

River drama

Torrential rain falls on the area at the top of the valley.
This causes flooding at the bottom.
Describe the scene.
Suggest how the people in the village cope with the floods.

PUZZLE PAGE

Ask your teacher for a copy of this puzzle.
Fit each of the words in the list into the puzzle.

HOUSE	DEPTH	GHOST	ALREADY	ERROR
ATTAIN	SEAT	REPLY	ICE-CUBE	ITEM
BEAN	GENERAL	DYED	TERRIBLE	OLIVE
OPERATE	STOP	LESSEN	THOUGH	LYRIC
ANOTHER	EDIT	INSIDE	VENTILATE	EMPTY
ENDURE	PETROL	TYPE	ORANGE	

Fit the words clockwise so that the last two letters
of each word become the first two letters of the next.

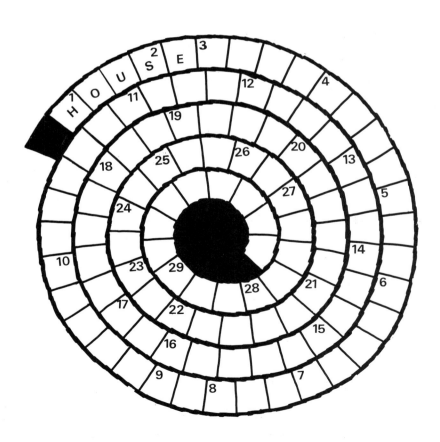

51

Rat 鼠

New Year celebrations in Trafalgar Square

A haggis

Ox 牛

NEW YEAR CELEBRATIONS

For many people, New Year's Day is on January 1st.
It is the first day of the calendar and for many people
it is a holiday. It is a time for parties and fun.

In London, thousands of people meet in Trafalgar Square.
From the square they can hear Big Ben 'ring in' the New Year.

In Scotland, New Year is called Hogmanay.
It is the time to eat haggis.
This is a kind of boiled meat pudding.

In China, New Year's Day falls at a different time
each year. The holiday comes on a day between January 21st
and February 19th. The Chinese name their years
after different animals. First comes the year of the rat.
For example, 1984 was a year of the rat.
Next comes the year of the ox. Then comes the year
of the tiger. This is followed by the year of the hare.
After this come years named after the dragon,
snake, horse, sheep, monkey, cockerel and dog.
Last of all comes the year of the pig.
When the year of the pig is over, it is time to start
with the year of the rat again.

Tiger 虎

Rabbit 兔

Dragon 龍

Snake 蛇

Read the passage, then answer these questions.

1   When do people in Britain celebrate
    New Year's Day?

2   Where do many Londoners meet
    on New Year's Eve?
    a   Buckingham Palace
    b   Trafalgar Square
    c   Tower of London

3   What are New Year celebrations called
    in Scotland?

4   The traditional food at the Scottish New Year is:
    a   jam pudding
    b   haggis
    c   pancakes

5   What is a haggis?

6   Between which dates do the Chinese
    celebrate New Year?

7   The Chinese give an animal name to each year.
    Which year follows the 'year of the rat'?

8   Holiday, Hogmanay, haggis, and horse are words
    from the passage. Write them in alphabetical order.

9   Knew and new are words which sound
    the same but are spelt differently.
    Find words in the passage which sound
    the same as the ones below but are spelt differently.
    a   wring   c   there
    b   too   d   here

10 Which word or words in the passage mean:
    a   not the same
    b   came after
    c   begin?

Pig

Dog

Rooster

 Horse

 Sheep

 Monkey

Choose the best meaning for each of these words.

TENDER
a   clear
b   hard
c   soft

SLENDER
a   quiet
b   quick
c   long and thin

GRAZE
a   sleep lightly
b   eat grass
c   to lift up

UNCOMFORTABLE
a   unhappy
b   unwilling
c   uneasy

DISPLAY
a   hide
b   show
c   break

DISASTER
a   great mishap
b   happy event
c   heavy load

AID
a   help
b   repair
c   break

ECHO
a   repeated sound
b   loud bang
c   steady beat

FLEXIBLE
a   very strong
b   easily bent
c   soft and smooth

RECOUNT
a   tell a lie
b   repay
c   relate an event

RUMBLE
a   a low, heavy noise
b   broken bits
c   evil remarks

FORBIDDEN
a   not happy
b   not clear
c   not allowed

Write twelve sentences containing the words in capital letters.
Use a different word in each sentence.

Arrange these words in alphabetical order:

<u>sacred</u>   saddle   <u>sample</u>   <u>satchel</u>   saw

<u>salad</u>   sand   saucer   Saxon   say

safe   sail   <u>sardine</u>   <u>savage</u>   satin

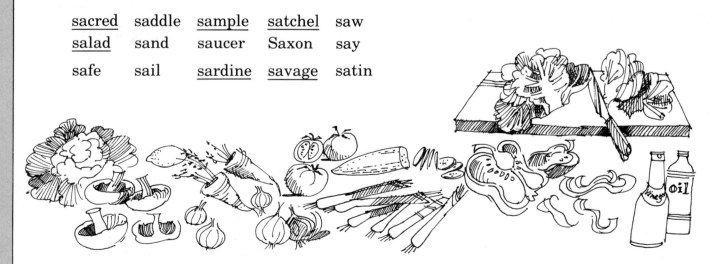

Use your dictionary to find the meanings of the words underlined.

ITS and IT'S

Remember **its** means belonging.

　The bird built its nest among the heather.

It's is a short way of writing **it is**

　I am sure it's going to rain.

Copy and complete these sentences using <u>its</u> or <u>it's</u>.

1　. . . . . very dark outside.
2　The leopard cannot change . . . . spots.
3　Switch on the power and see if . . . . working.
4　Look carefully and see if the bird has broken
　. . . . . wing.
5　If the car fails . . . . test I will sell it.
6　. . . . . not very far to the bus stop.

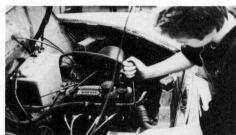

WAS and WERE

Remember **was** is used when you are speaking or writing
　about one person or thing.

The dog was barking in the night.

Were is used when you are speaking or writing
about more than one person or thing.

My sisters were both good at tennis.

Write sentences starting with these words.

1　John was　　　6　Were you
2　They were　　7　Was he
3　I was　　　　8　Were they
4　You were　　9　Was I
5　They were　　10　Billy and I

Fear and Fright

WRITING WORK 1   ASSIGNMENT 66

Almost everyone has been frightened at some time. Fear often comes as a result of some unexpected happening – being on a mountain when fog and mist suddenly appear, being cut off by the incoming tide, or developing cramp while swimming. Some people say that they have been frightened by mysterious happenings.

They have been afraid because they heard footsteps on a landing or a piano playing in an empty room.

Here are some words about fear and fright.

Copy them into your book.

horror   terrifying
scares   dreadful
terror   spine-chilling

WRITING WORK 2   ASSIGNMENT 67

Write about an experience you have had when you were very frightened.

WRITING WORK 3   ASSIGNMENT 68

Write a short story called THE INCIDENT OF TERROR.
Use some of the words from assignment 66 in your story.

PUZZLE PAGE

WORD DOMINOES

Ask your teacher for a copy of this puzzle.

Fit the words listed below into the puzzle.

Write each six letter word in a clockwise direction starting in the numbered square.

Whenever dominoes meet, the letters in the adjoining squares match each other.

The first word has been written in for you.

ACTION	AFFECT	ARTIST	ASPIRE	REALLY	REGION
CHIEFS	COBALT	CORNET	CATERS	SENTRY	SITTER
ESSAYS	FALLEN	FLEETS	FOREST	RETURN	UTTERS
GROUPS	IGNORE	LETTER	SELDOM	TABLES	

RADAR

Comprehension

Radar is among the great inventions of our time.
It is used during darkness to guide ships safely
to port. It helps planes land and take off when airport
conditions are poor.

Radar is a British invention. It was first invented
by Robert Watson-Watt and other British scientists.
The first chain of radar stations was built
in Britain in 1936.

Radar makes use of radio waves. Radio waves move
through the air in straight lines. Their speed is known.
The waves sent out from a radar station continue
in a straight line until they hit an object in their path.
This object may be a ship or plane, for example.
The waves then bounce back to the radar station.
The time this takes is recorded. From these recordings
the position, direction and speed of the object
can be calculated.

Radar is used in the defence of Britain. It helped Britain
defeat the Germans in the Battle of Britain during
the Second World War.

Robert Watson-Watt was a Scotsman. He died in 1973.

Inside a radar station

Read the passage, then answer these questions.

1 What nationality was Robert Watson-Watt?
   a Irish
   b Welsh
   c Scottish
   d English

2 What did Robert Watson-Watt invent?
   a television
   b radar
   c electricity

3 What does the passage say about the movement
of radio waves?
Do they move:
   a in circles
   b in straight lines
   c in zig-zags?

4 When was the first chain of radar stations built?

5 Name two ways in which radar is used.

6 In which battle did the use of radar
help decide who won?

7 Which two nations were at war when this battle
was fought?

8 With the help of a dictionary write different sentences
to show the meanings of these words:
   a conditions
   b calculated
   c invention

9 Find the word or words in the passage
which mean:
   a the place where aeroplanes land
   b show the way
   c noted

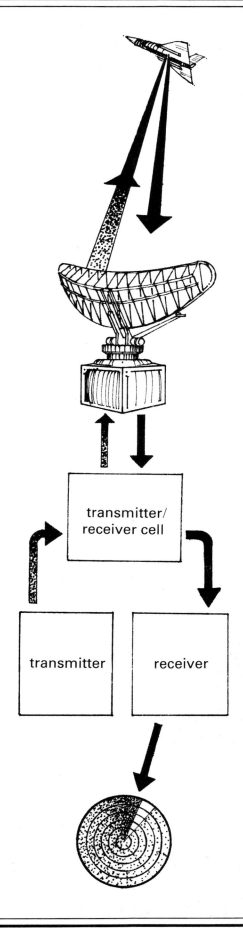

WORD WORK 1

1 Choose the best meaning for each of these words.

EXTEND
a to cut short
b to lenthen
c to explain

JEALOUS
a mean
b envious
c fussy

CONFIRM
a to cancel
b to make certain of
c to prove wrong

IMMEDIATE
a important
b in the future
c at once

SURRENDER
a to give in
b to carry on
c to avoid

NEGLECT
a to look after
b to damage
c to take no care of

WORD WORK 2

The word 'lock' has two meanings. 1 A lock is a part of a canal.

2 A lock is used to fasten a door.

 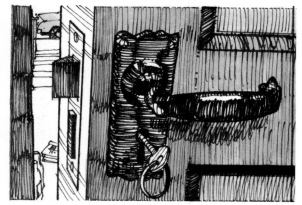

Here are other words which have two meanings.

race, bear, kite, light, fencing

**Write sentences to show you know the two meanings
of each word.**

WORD WORK 3

Arrange these words in dictionary order.

ebony enlarge echo eternal equal egg evade

elbow eject eel embark edge enlist epic

effort eight each equal erode exalt

Use your dictionary to find the meanings of the words underlined.
Write sentences using a different word in each sentence.

LANGUAGE WORK 1

Ten of the words in this list are proper nouns.
They should begin with a capital letter.

Copy the list. Underline the proper nouns. Use capital letters.

thursday daisy chicken wales easter
orange buttercup lake biscuit snowdon
wife july david sweets chocolate blackberry
janet apple book pen pencil perth cardiff
matterhorn wine cheese cream butter fish

LANGUAGE WORK 2

Write down names of three of each of these:

1 towns	2 countries	3 counties
4 rivers	5 mountains	6 months
7 days of the week	8 famous people	9 school subjects
10 people in your class		

LANGUAGE WORK 3

Copy and correct these sentences.
Mr and Mrs Johnson (were, was) shown where to sit.
Carl (was, were) best man at Jane's wedding.
If (its, it's) too cold we will play indoors.
The cuckoo has little regard for (it's, its) young.
(It's, Its) a shame if (its, it's) leg is broken.
The criminals (did, done) a great deal of damage.
It seemed that (their, there) was no one left in the building.

LANGUAGE WORK 4

Copy and correct this passage.

nigel and ian went on holiday together
they left home and met at the bus station
nigel had to walk down wilson avenue
then along the high street to get to
the bus station ian had only to walk
through monk's park they left the
blackwood bus station by bus and
went to cardiff

from cardiff the two boys took
the train to reading here their holiday
really began it was saturday they
hired a boat and sailed down
the thames to london

on their voyage they saw
the houses of parliament
big ben the tower of london
hms belfast and the cutty sark

LANGUAGE WORK 5

Make suitable endings for each of the phrases with these nouns. Use a different noun each time.

ice	mule	nails	mustard	lightning
eel	lead	giant	thunder	cucumber
fox	ox	daisy	butter	berry

1   as quick as ....
2   as strong as an ....
3   as cold as ....
4   as stubborn as a ....
5   as keen as ....
6   as tall as a ....
7   as hard as ....
8   as fresh as a ....
9   as heavy as ....
10   as cunning as a ....
11   as loud as......................
12   as slippery as an ....
13   as soft as ....
14   as cool as a ....
15   as brown as a ....

WRITING WORK 1

Here are the opening paragraphs of three stories.
Choose one of them and continue the story.

It was the evening of Hallowe'en.
David and his sister Ann were walking
past the Old Rectory. 'Look David,'
whispered Ann. 'Look at the attic
window. I can see a face staring out.'
'Don't be daft,' said David,
'No one has lived there for ten years.'

WRITING WORK 2

Roy and Margaret were walking along
the promenade. The wind was blowing,
the waves breaking over the railings.
Suddenly, a bright red flare appeared
over the headland …

WRITING WORK 3

It was Thursday, second lesson.
I was doing some maths. First,
it sounded like a clicking noise
in the distance. Soon, it was clear
as the unmistakable noise of an
approaching helicopter. The 'chopper'
came nearer, nearer, hovered above
the school and landed on the tennis courts.
To my amazement out stepped …

The British Grenadiers

Every day hundreds of people can be seen outside
Buckingham Palace watching the Changing of the Guard.
The Guards are the Queen's Household Troops, formed
to look after the Royal Family.

In the Army the Foot Guards are part of the Household
Division. The senior Regiment of Foot Guards
is called the Grenadier Guards. They are called
Foot Guards to distinguish them from the mounted
or Horse Guards.

The Regiment was formed in 1660. This was in the reign
of King Charles II. The soldiers were known as
the First Foot Guards.

The First Foot Guards fought at the Battle of Waterloo,
helping to defeat Napoleon's Army. Napoleon
had soldiers called Grenadiers. They were called this
because in battle they threw grenades at the enemy.
The British First Foot Guards defeated the French
Grenadiers and afterwards took their name and bearskin cap.

The Grenadier's uniform is similar to that of the other
Guards Regiments. He wears blue trousers, a scarlet
tunic and a black bearskin cap. A Grenadier's buttons
are equally spaced.

Read the passage, then answer these questions.

1   Where in London are you likely to see
    the Grenadier Guards?

2   By what name were the First Foot Guards known?

3   The First Foot Guards were formed in the reign of:
    a   Elizabeth I
    b   George IV
    c   Charles II

4   The First Foot Guards took the name 'Grenadiers'
    after the battle of:
    a   Britain
    b   Waterloo
    c   Hastings

5   How are the buttons arranged on the tunic
    of a grenadier?

6   In the passage a 'bearskin' means:
    a   soldier without clothes
    b   a tall hat
    c   a polar bear's coat

7   What word or words in the passage mean:
    a   uniform coat
    b   tell the difference between
    c   safe-guard?

8   <u>Fought</u> is the past tense of the verb to <u>fight.</u>
    Give the past tense of:
    a   seek
    b   sing
    c   go

DESCRIBING WORDS — ADJECTIVES

A word that describes or tells you more about a noun is called an adjective.
The <u>grey</u> mare stood still as the <u>young</u> horseman
put on its <u>shining</u> harness.

Copy these sentences into your book. Underline the adjectives.
1   The thick soup was drunk eagerly by the hungry
    children.
2   The hot sun turned the brown earth into a fine
    dust.
3   It took three policemen to arrest the struggling
    man.
4   My mother wore a straw hat, white dress and red
    shoes and carried a bunch of spring flowers
    at the wedding reception.
5   The yellow dandelion is considered by many
    to be an unsightly weed, but really it is
    a colourful flower.

Look at the pictures.

**Write two sentences describing what the person
in each picture is doing.**
Use at least two adjectives in each of your sentences.

Form an adjective from each of these nouns.
The first one has been done for you.

gold – golden

wool	silk	anger
slip	excite	spot
freeze	beauty	stripe
mist	sleep	isolate

Now write sentences using these adjectives.
Use a different adjective in each sentence.

**From the adjectives on the right select the one
which has a different meaning from the
one in BLOCK LETTERS.**

HUGE   vast, big, colossal, enormous, small
WISE   clever, sensible, learned, stupid
FOOLISH   stupid, ignorant, happy, silly, unwise
HOT   warm, scorching, cool, boiling
LONELY   deserted, busy, single, friendless, solitary

big *small* HUGE **VAST**

Play the adjective game – My aunty's cat.
Join together into a group of two or three. Take turns.
The first player makes up a sentence using an adjective
beginning with the letter 'A'.
  For example: My aunty's cat is an awful cat.

The next follows but this time the adjective begins
with the letter 'B'.
  For example: My aunty's cat is a beautiful cat.

Continue until most letters of the alphabet have been used.

►The Father Of The Modern Computer

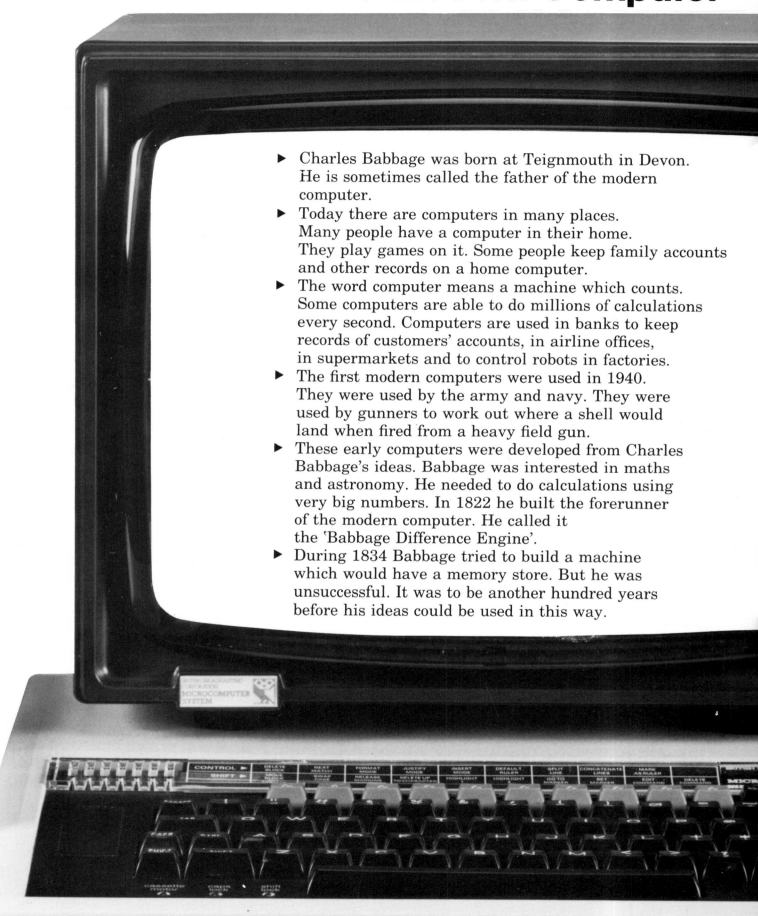

- ► Charles Babbage was born at Teignmouth in Devon. He is sometimes called the father of the modern computer.
- ► Today there are computers in many places. Many people have a computer in their home. They play games on it. Some people keep family accounts and other records on a home computer.
- ► The word computer means a machine which counts. Some computers are able to do millions of calculations every second. Computers are used in banks to keep records of customers' accounts, in airline offices, in supermarkets and to control robots in factories.
- ► The first modern computers were used in 1940. They were used by the army and navy. They were used by gunners to work out where a shell would land when fired from a heavy field gun.
- ► These early computers were developed from Charles Babbage's ideas. Babbage was interested in maths and astronomy. He needed to do calculations using very big numbers. In 1822 he built the forerunner of the modern computer. He called it the 'Babbage Difference Engine'.
- ► During 1834 Babbage tried to build a machine which would have a memory store. But he was unsuccessful. It was to be another hundred years before his ideas could be used in this way.

Read the passage then answer these questions.

1 Who is sometimes called the father of the computer?

2 Where was Charles Babbage born?

3 What does the word computer mean?

4 What does the expression 'father of the modern computer' mean?

5 Babbage was a man interested in:
    a cookery and needlework
    b maths and astronomy
    c English and French

6 What did Babbage call his first computers?

7 The first modern computer was built in:
    a 1910
    b 1940
    c 1985

8 How can a computer be used in the home?

9 Does the word RECORD, as used in the passage mean:
    a a disc recording
    b recording tape
    c written lists

10 The opposite of OLD as used in the passage is MODERN.
What is the opposite of:
    a few
    b to take off
    c successful

| USING ADJECTIVES TO MAKE COMPARISONS |

Some adjectives can be used to make comparisons.
Look at the picture of the three boys.

Notice: Bill is tall. John is taller than Bill.
David is the tallest.

In the first sentence there is no comparison.

In the second sentence there is a comparison
between two people – John and Bill.

In the third sentence there is a comparison
between more than two people – John, Bill, David.

Copy and complete this table of comparison.

No comparison	Comparison between two	Comparison of more than two	No comparison	Comparison between two	Comparison of more than two
big			hot		
	faster			colder	
		latest			longest
	older			thinner	
		smallest	fat		
large					shortest
	nearer		rich		
		greenest	dry		
fair				lighter	
	cooler			heavier	
		warmest	strong		
dark					weakest

Although some adjectives make comparisons by adding
'er' or 'est', others make comparisons by using completely
different words.

good	better	best
little	less	least
many	more	most

Some other adjectives make comparisons by placing the words
'more' or 'most' in front.

beautiful　more beautiful　most beautiful

**Write the three comparative forms for each of these
adjectives.**

neat	comfortable	kind	new	fair
sweet	little	merry	early	desirable
valuable	expensive	hot	strong	good

many　　　more　　　most

LANGUAGE WORK 3　　　　　　　　　　　　　　**ASSIGNMENT 79**

Copy these sentences into your book.
Use the correct comparison word taken from those
in the brackets.

1　Which is the (lighter　lightest) of the two boxes?
2　John is the (taller　tallest　tall) of the four boys.
3　Mary thought the green dress was the (best　better)
　　of the two in the window.
4　The parcel is the (heavier　heaviest) of the six
　　in the van.
5　We thought Sandra the (nice　nicer　nicest) of the three girls.
6　I am reading a (funny　funniest　funnier) book.
7　Robert had the (less　least　lesser) amount of money.
8　The (smaller　smaller　smallest) bottle of perfume
　　was the more expensive of the two on the counter.

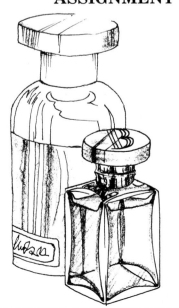

WRITING A FORMAL LETTER

Here is an example of a formal letter:

Tel: Blackwood 2167

28 High Street
Blackwood
Westhamptonshire
BD3 2LA

The Manager
Superwools Ltd
South Street
Bridgetown
Westhamptonshire
BN5 3KT

6th March 1987

Dear Sir,

I am writing to complain about a sweater that I bought from your shop in Blackwood on Saturday 2nd March. I followed the instructions on the label and put it in a hot wash, but it has shrunk.

I am enclosing the sweater with this letter. Please could you send me a replacement?

Yours faithfully,

David Smith

Notice that the letter divides into eight parts.

1 **Your telephone number**
   This goes in the top left-hand corner.

2 **Your address.**
   Either the block or the indented form may be used.

Block form	**Indented form**
28 High Street	28 High Street
Blackwood	Blackwood
Westhamptonshire	Westhamptonshire
BD3 2LA	BD3 2LA

3 **The date**
   Write the day and name of the month followed by the year.

4 **The person you are writing to**
   Always write to the head of the company.
   If you do not know whether it is a man or a woman,
   write to the Manager.

5 **The name of the Company**
Beneath the title of the person in the company
write the name and address of the company.

6 **Title**
When you write to a person in a company, use
the person's name, if you know it.
    Dear Mr Brown   Dear Mrs Barton   Dear Ms Smith
If you do not know the name of the person
use Dear Sir or Madam

7 **The substance**
Be brief.
Say what your letter is about and what it is you want done.

8 **The ending**
If you have written to a person by name end your letter
    Yours sincerely
If you have begun by using Dear Sir end your letter
    Yours faithfully

9 **Signature**
Write your name clearly in full.

Copy the letter and notes into your book.

ASSIGNMENT 81

These advertisements appeared in the Bridgnorth Advertiser.
Write a reply to one of them.

DRUMMER
REQUIRED
For Jazz Club
**Commercial Street
Bridgnorth BN4 SPB**
Please send applications
to Secretary at
above address.

**FATHER'S DAY
TIES**
Embroidered with
initials or Christian
name in navy,
brown or burgundy.
Write stating name,
address, first and
second colour
choice and initials,
or name required
to:–

**3 St Nicholas Court
Bridgnorth
BN5 6NT**

Enclose cheque P/O for
£3.50 (inclusive p + p)

ASSIGNMENT 82

**How many words can you make from the letters
contained in the words:**

BABBAGE, COMPUTER INVENTOR

Mount Vesuvius is in Italy. It is near the modern city of Naples.

Vesuvius is a volcano. For most of the time the mountain looks asleep. However, underneath it is very much alive. The mountain is watched by scientists day and night. They record the rumblings that go on deep inside the volcano. The scientists are there to give an early warning to the thousands of people who live in villages at the foot of the mountain.

However, there was no early warning for the people of Pompeii in AD79. At that time, Pompeii was a busy city nestling at the foot of Vesuvius. August 24th was a holiday and most people were enjoying themselves at the games and races.

Without warning Vesuvius exploded. Within minutes the city was covered with a layer of red hot ash several feet deep. Few escaped. Men, women, animals, plants, everything was covered with the stinking ash. It was as if life stood still.

Years later Pompeii was excavated. The diggings showed what life was like in a Roman city nearly two thousand years ago. Many of the things that were found can be seen in the museum at Naples.

ITALY

Naples
Vesuvius

The Buried City of Mount Vesuvius

SICILY

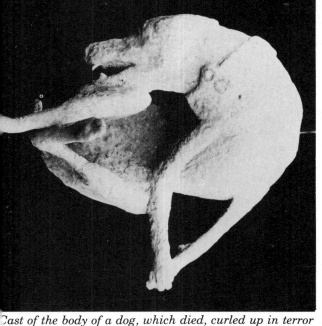

Cast of the body of a dog, which died, curled up in terror

Read the passage, then answer the questions.

1   Which country is Mount Vesuvius in?

2   At the foot of the mountain there once stood
    a city called:
    a St Albans
    b Pompeii
    c Paris

3   Mount Vesuvius is a volcano.
    When did it erupt, destroying Pompeii?

4   Where can articles excavated from the city's ruins
    be seen?

5   Scientists continuously observe Mount Vesuvius
    to:
    a enjoy the view
    b watch the fruit on the trees ripening
    c see if there are signs of another eruption

6   Find from reference books the names of two other
    volcanoes.

7   Italy is a proper noun.
    Find three other proper nouns in the passage.

8   Find the words in the passage which mean:
    a dug out
    b burst out
    c observed

9   AD stands for the Latin words Anno Domini.
    It means 'in the year of the Lord', or 'After Christ'.
    What does the abbreviation BC mean?

A room in the Villa of Mysteries, reconstructed for the Pompeii Exhibition

WORD WORK 1

wriggled obvious supper veil
Thursday ribbon quarrel threatened

Change the words underlined in each sentence for one of the above words.

1 The snake <u>twisted and turned</u> across the path.

2 The lady pulled down her <u>net</u> over her face.

3 The bully <u>promised to hurt</u> the little boy.

4 There is a market here on <u>the fourth day of the week.</u>

5 We had <u>the last meal of the day</u> at ten o'clock.

6 Mary tied up her hair with a <u>long narrow piece of material.</u>

7 Karl and Nigel had a <u>furious disagreement.</u>

8 The answer to the problem was <u>clear to me.</u>

WORD WORK 2

Match each of these words with its meaning.

Use your dictionary if you need
to find the meanings of these words.

TRAGEDY	to arouse hostility
DECREPIT	careless
LANGUID	to insult someone
ANTAGONISE	drink
SPRIGHTLY	weak
REMISS	a serious disaster
ADHERE	lively and brisk
AQUATIC	prompt
BEVERAGE	old and feeble
PUNCTUAL	to stick to
AFFRONT	living in water

WORD WORK 3

Find one word for each of these phrases.
All the words you need begin with the letter **L**.

a   to allow   b   to be without
c   to guide   d   to jump over
e   to lie in wait   f   to fill up a truck
g   to walk lamely   h   to be very fond of

Use each of the words in a different sentence.

WORD WORK 4

From each group of words choose two words of similar meaning.

1   relinquish abandon repent
2   perish worry perturb
3   smooth conceal hide
4   regular regal kingly
5   sure certain probably
6   powerful possible potent
7   doctor medicine drugs
8   region area metre
9   mat rug plastic

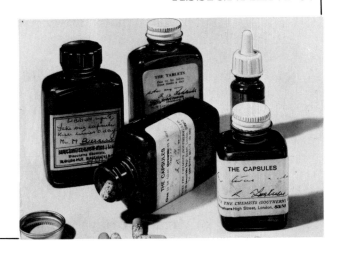

WORD WORK 5

History is the study of the past.
Find out what these subjects are about.
Use your dictionary if necessary.

ANATOMY
BIOLOGY
BOTANY
ZOOLOGY
GEOGRAPHY
PHYSICS
ARCHAEOLOGY
GEOLOGY

COLOURFUL SAYINGS

Sometimes we use short expressions which make
what we are saying more colourful.

Here are some of them.
a   a storm in a teacup
b   a busman's holiday
c   a white elephant
d   a red herring
e   a black sheep
f   a rough diamond
g   a fish out of water
h   a flash in the pan
i   a bull in a china shop

Copy each of the sayings into your book.
Match each saying with what you think is the best explanation
chosen from the list below.

1   a gift that is quite useless
2   something which takes attention from the main topic
3   great excitement over a very small matter
4   a holiday where the person does the same
    thing as when at work
5   a worthless character
6   a clumsy, destructive person
7   someone who is out of place
8   a good hearted person but with rough manners
9   a showy start which quickly comes to nothing

WRITING WORK 2   **ASSIGNMENT 90**

Write sentences.
Use each of the expressions in a separate sentence.

PUZZLE PAGE

Ask your teacher for a copy of this puzzle.

ASSIGNMENT 91

Look at the list of words at the side of the puzzle.
Can you fit them into the grid?
Start with the 10 letter word.

10 LETTERS
undertaken

9 LETTERS
situation   tentacles

8 LETTERS
ailments   holidays

7 LETTERS
applaud   dialled
defence

6 LETTERS
really   neater
armies

5 LETTERS
gully   knead   added
means   aisle   drown

4 LETTERS
star   rook   lime
wood   dawn   mate
trot

3 LETTERS
ere   dim   are   ace
tea   ask   his   got
sit   all   asp   inn
lap   nil

Samuel Pepys

Samuel Pepys Esq.ˢ Secretary to the Admiralty.
From an Original by Sir Godfrey Kneller.

Some people like to keep a diary. This is a record of
what happens each day to the person who keeps the diary.
Diaries of well-known people are sometimes published.
When this happens we can read accounts of the events,
big and small, in their lives. One such diary is by Samuel Pepys.

Pepys was born in London in 1633 and lived there for seventy years.
He began to write his famous diary in 1660.
In it Pepys tells of two famous events.

1665 was the year of the Great Plague. The plague disease
was carried by fleas on rats. Thousands of people died.
Pepys tells of dead people lying unburied in the streets
and of terrible smells.

In 1666 Pepys recorded the Great Fire of London.
It started in a baker's shop. He says how he hurried to tell
King Charles II about the fire. It was soon completely
out of control. There were no fire engines like ours.
The only way to stop the fire spreading further was to pull down
buildings. Then the fire could not jump the gap. A large part
of London was destroyed.

In 1669 Pepys had to give up writing his diary because he thought
he was going blind. He did not in fact become blind, but he never
kept his diary again.

Read the passage, then answer these questions.

1   What is a diary?

2   Where was Samuel Pepys born?

3   How old was he when he started his diary?

4   In 1665 Pepys described:
    a the Great Plague
    b the Wars of the Roses
    c the Great Fire of London

5   What big event did Pepys describe in 1666?

6   Where did the Fire of London start?

7   We buy bread from a baker's shop.
   Where do we buy:
    a medicine
    b meat
    c sweets and chocolates

8   Why did Pepys give up his diary?
   Was it because:
    a it was full
    b he was becoming blind
    c he was bored with it

9   The word 'lives' means more than one life.
   Give the plural for:
    a knife
    b shelf
    c calf

10   Which words in the passage mean:
    a started
    b tell
    c occurs?

Coal seller

Old coats suits and coats seller

New river-water seller

MORE WORK WITH VERBS

Copy these sentences into your book.
Underline the verb in each sentence.

1   I heard a tiger in the forest.
2   Jane walked home from school.
3   We will watch the match on television.
4   Margaret is enjoying her curry.
5   An eagle is flying overhead.
6   We will leave school in July.
7   David drank two cans of coke.
8   Sian is making her wedding dress.

LANGUAGE WORK 2

**Replace the verb in each of these sentences
with one of similar meaning.**

1   His father asked him to help.
2   The builders obtained a long ladder.
3   The noise frightened the animals.
4   The message was concealed in the prisoner's food.
5   I have almost completed the painting.
6   My friend dislikes country style music.

LANGUAGE WORK 3

**Replace the verb in each of these sentences
with one of opposite meaning.**

1   My friend has just arrived.
2   I like beans and chips.
3   Amin's work always pleased his teacher.
4   The children were punished for their behaviour.
5   During the battle the troops advanced
    to a new position.
6   The climbers ascended the mountain with great care.

This signpost gives information to holiday makers about river cruises.

Look at the picture, then answer the questions.

1   What is the name of the river along which the cruise is to go?

2   In which holiday town would you see this sign?

3   If you were on a half-day visit would going on this cruise be a good idea?

4   What time does the cruise leave?

5   What time does it return?

6   How long are you on the water?

7   What important information is missing from the notice?

8   Which word describes the Devon coast? What other word could have been chosen?

9   Will there be a chance to see another Devon seaside town?

10 What town will it be and how long will the passengers have there?

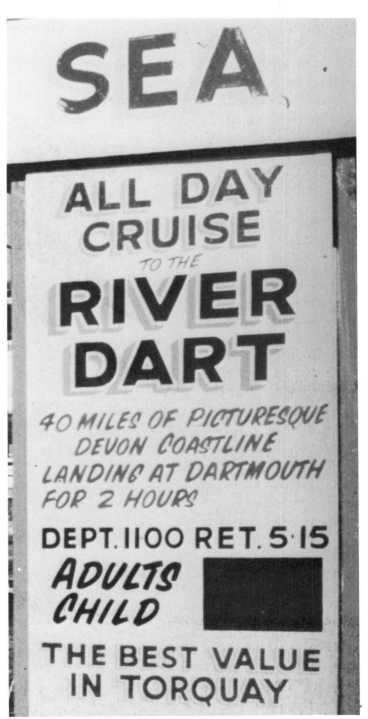

KEEPING A DIARY

Many people like to keep a diary.
A diary is a daily account of the events,
thoughts and happenings which are part of your life.

Here are some of the things written about in a diary.

1 things done   2 family happenings   3 friends   4 relations
5 games   6 TV programmes   7 national events 8 books read

**Use these headings to
write the diary of your life
over the past seven days.**

WRITING WORK 2   **ASSIGNMENT 98**

Think back to last Christmas.
**Write your diary from the morning of Christmas Eve
to the morning after Boxing Day.**

WRITING WORK 3   **ASSIGNMENT 99**

These pictures will perhaps remind you of a holiday
abroad.
**Look at the pictures, then either write a diary of your holiday
or write a diary of an imaginary holiday abroad.**

PUZZLE PAGE

Ask your teacher for a copy of this puzzle.

This puzzle contains the twenty-five names of insects listed below.

ant	aphid	bee	beetle	spider
butterfly	caddis	caterpillar	cockroach	woodlouse
cricket	dragonfly	earwig	flea	toadhopper
grasshopper	hornet	ladybird	locust	wasp
louse	mosquito	moth	pondskater	waterboatman

Find each name

As you find each name write it in your book.

You can read like this: → ↓ ↘

W	O	O	D	L	O	U	S	E	A	S	T	U	Q	D
L	A	D	Y	B	I	R	D	B	T	S	H	O	P	R
C	N	T	B	A	L	M	V	U	R	M	O	T	H	A
C	A	T	E	R	P	I	L	L	A	R	R	D	Q	G
E	F	F	E	R	U	W	V	B	P	R	N	S	T	O
K	F	L	V	W	B	C	R	I	C	K	E	T	M	N
J	G	O	E	X	U	O	A	C	O	W	T	X	O	F
I	H	C	Y	A	T	C	A	N	D	N	Y	H	S	L
L	O	U	S	E	T	K	S	T	T	I	M	G	Q	Y
J	Z	S	A	X	E	R	P	E	M	L	Z	F	U	D
W	K	T	Y	B	R	O	I	K	E	A	R	W	I	G
Z	A	L	G	R	F	A	D	A	P	J	N	R	T	N
A	S	S	M	H	L	C	E	O	B	P	E	I	O	B
A	G	R	P	N	Y	H	R	C	A	D	D	I	S	E
P	O	N	D	S	K	A	T	E	R	O	C	H	C	E
H	A	S	T	O	A	D	H	O	P	P	E	R	P	T
I	S	H	O	P	T	L	Y	A	D	G	D	Q	B	L
D	G	R	A	S	S	H	O	P	P	E	R	F	X	E
D	R	A	G	R	A	D	O	E	T	E	R	B	L	Y

The English Ship Swallower

COMPREHENSION

The English Channel is one of the world's busiest
shipping lanes. Five miles off the Kent coast in the middle
of the channel is one of the world's greatest shipping hazards.
The hazard is a mountain of sand. It is twelve miles
long and about five miles wide. It lies just beneath
the surface of the sea. The sand mountain is known as
the Goodwin Sands. It is a constant danger to shipping.
Over the years dozens of ships have sailed into the sands
and been sucked down, never to be seen again.
Old sailors call the sands the 'English ship swallower'.

The hazards is made more difficult for sailors because
it is always changing its position. Although three lightships
and ten buoys mark the position of the sands, ships still sail into
them. At low tide, the sands sometimes show part
of their grim contents. The mast of the North Eastern Victory
sometimes appears above the water. This ship sank in 1944.
Holiday-makers sometimes see the mast as they cross
to France aboard the cross-channel ferries.

The Goodwin sands are named after Earl Godwine.
He was the father of King Harold. Harold was one of the first
kings of England, who was killed at the battle of Hastings in 1066.

**Read the passage,
then answer these questions.**

1   Where is the English Channel?

2   The Goodwin Sands are:
    a a famous beach
    b a dangerous sand bank
    c a holiday camp

3   Why are the Goodwin Sands dangerous?

4   What marks the position
    of the Sands for shipping?

5   When are holiday-makers likely to see
    wrecked ships?

6   Earl Goodwin was:
    a Father of King Harold
    b Husband of Queen Victoria
    c Son of Henry VIII

7   What is the North Eastern Victory?

8   Kent is an English county.
    Put the names of these counties
    in alphabetical order.
    Essex   Avon
    Gwent   Berkshire
    Cumbria Sussex

9   Buoy and boy sound the same,
    but have different meanings.
    Find the words in the passage
    with the same sound as:
    a won
    b bean
    c see

10 Find the words in the passage which
    mean the same as:
    a danger
    b boats carrying people and cars
    c under

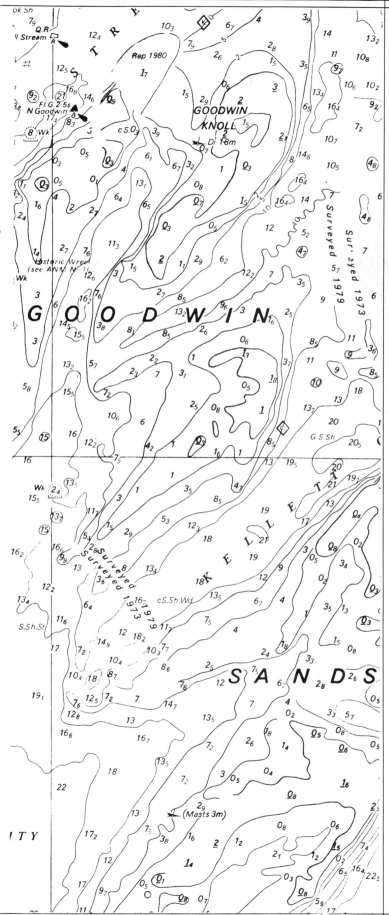

WORD WORK 1

Copy each group of words into your book.
In each group underline two words which are similar
in meaning to the word in CAPITAL LETTERS.

LARGE   enormous round small big
WET   damp dark dank dusty dry
CARPET   rug mat pillow sheet
ROAD   stream street field avenue
HOUSE   factory shop bungalow cottage

WORD WORK 2

compliment ransacked debris peeped
ventilated fragrance thrust moment

**Replace the underlined phrases with the right words
from the list.**

1 Jean made a <u>nice remark</u> about Susan's dress.
2 After the explosion the floor was covered
   with <u>broken glass, bricks and rubbish.</u>
3 The flowers in the field had a nice <u>smell.</u>
4 It only took a <u>very short length of time</u> for the police to come.
5 Janet <u>looked through the keyhole</u> at the people
   in the room.
6 The knight <u>strongly forced</u> his sword into his enemy.
7 The fan <u>allowed fresh air to enter</u> the room.
8 The thieves <u>completely disturbed and upset</u>
   the room and its contents.

WORD WORK 3

Match each of the words on the left with its meaning.

minute	participate
offend	quarrel
request	scarlet
tamper	vertical
undertone	yearn
withhold	

displease	to take part in
to ask for	brilliant red
to long for	very small
an angry dispute	upright
in a low voice	to keep back
to interfere with	

LANGUAGE WORK 1

Copy and correct these sentences.

1 Margaret was the eldest of the two sisters.
2 David was the younger of the three brothers.
3 The cold grew worser as the snow fell.
4 Nigel bought the more expensive jacket of the three in the shop.

LANGUAGE WORK 2

Replace the verb in each of the following sentences with one of opposite meaning.

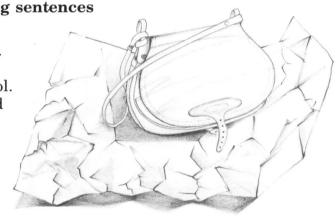

1 The train has just arrived at the station.
2 Amanda won the race.
3 I found a pound coin on the way to school.
4 The big factory at the bottom of the road has just closed.
5 Sindi has bought her bicycle.
6 Jack caused an accident in the gym.

LANGUAGE WORK 3

Copy these sentences into your book.
Underline the adjectives in each one.

1 The great eagle could be seen flying in the clear, blue sky.
2 The express train thundered through the tiny station on its way to the busy city.
3 The yellow sails of the shining yacht could be seen across the silent harbour.
4 Colin hopes to get a permanent job in the new car factory.
5 The strong smell of vegetable soup gave the hungry boys hope of a good meal.

WRITING WORK 1

Write in full: your name
your address
your date of birth
the day of the week
the month of the year
the name of your school
the name of your doctor
the address of the doctor's surgery

December 1986 WEEK 1 WEEK 2 M

29 *Visiting Gran and Grandpa*

30 *Sales start*

31 *New Year's Eve party at Susan's*

January 1987 New Year's Day Holiday (UK)
Holiday (Republic of Ireland)
1

WRITING WORK 2

Write your diary for the last four evenings.
Write at least five sentences about each evening's thoughts and activities.

WRITING WORK 3

```
CARDIFF CYCLE CENTRE
      Raleigh Cycles
        From £78
         *   *   *
        No deposit
     After sales service
         *   *   *
   Available while stocks
            last
            *
    28 Queens Street
  CARDIFF   CFY 2RX.
```

This advertisement was seen in the SOUTH WALES ECHO on Thursday December 14th.

Write a letter to the Cardiff Cycle Centre ordering one of the cycles.

Explain: No deposit
From £78
After sales service
While stocks last

WRITING WORK 4

Here are four expressions:
1 to hit below the belt
2 to kick up a fuss
3 to get into hot water
4 to put the cart before the horse.

Here are their meanings:
a to cause a row
b to do things in the wrong order
c to do things unfairly
d to get into trouble.

Match each saying with its meaning.

Poetry page

Read this poem, then answer the questions.

The Oak is called the King of Trees,
The Aspen quivers in the breeze,
The Poplar grows up straight and tall,
The Pear-tree spreads along the wall,
The Sycamore gives pleasant shade,
The Willow droops in watery glade,
The Fir-tree useful timber gives,
The Beech amid the forest lives.

Sara Coldridge

1 Suggest a title for the poem.

2 According to the poem, which tree does the following?
    a gives shade on a sunny day
    b bears fruit
    c grows straight and tall
    d produces good timber

3 Which tree is described as the 'King of trees'?

4 The tree which spreads along the wall is the Pear-tree.
  Name two other fruit trees.

5 Name two other kinds of British tree not mentioned in the poem.

6 Explain these phrases:
    a quivers in the breeze
    b amid the forest

7 Answer 'yes' or 'no' to these statements.
    a The Beech grows in woods and forests.
    b The Willow tree likes dry sunny places.
    c The trunk of the Poplar tree makes excellent telegraph poles.

8 Oak, Beech, Ash and Poplar could be grouped under the heading TREES.

  What heading would you give these groups?
    a yacht catboat dinghy   b cars buses lorries
    c apples pears oranges   d potatoes carrots parsnips

1 **Arrange these words in alphabetical order.**

behold	delay	flag	halt	inhabit
café	malt	number	panther	lantern
bench	gear	ocean	reason	message
choice	jungle	mail	talent	union
abbey	embark	kerb	quake	scald
toast	wage	x-ray	yellow	vain
zebra	fish	queen	gone	hate

2 **Copy and punctuate these sentences.**

a   are you going to the disco
b   there are potatoes cabbages leeks onions and carrots on the market stall
c   david painted the ceiling of his bedroom white, the doors green and his desk yellow
d   it is a sunny day today
e   salina and hamid are going to coventry

3 **Match each of these words with its meaning.**

deduct	a crime
encounter	hardworking
miserable	to subtract
felony	unhappy
industrious	to meet face to face

4 **Write six sentences about your favourite sport.**

5 Write these groups of words in your book.
Underline the word in each group which is similar to the word in CAPITAL LETTERS.

HOUSE	greenhouse hut cottage castle
VIOLIN	cello guitar trumpet drum
CAR	ship aeroplane bus taxi
LION	tiger snake whale camel
RED	scarlet purple indigo orange

6 Write the words which mean the following:

a men who work on a ship
b a traveller in space
c an instrument for recording temperature
d a fertile place in a desert
e a field of fruit trees
f a doctor who performs operations

7 Explain these sayings:

a play with fire
b as the crow flies
c a flash in the pan
d to live from hand to mouth
e the lion's share
f from pillar to post

8 Match each of these sayings with its meaning.

Sayings
the apple of one's eye
the man in the street
lion-hearted
a rough diamond
a peppery individual

Meanings
someone who is hot tempered
someone who is especially dear
someone of great courage
someone who is kind hearted but of rough manners
an ordinary person

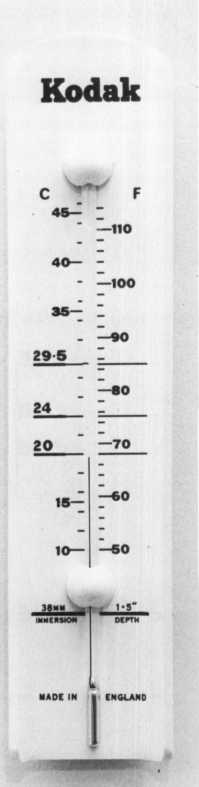

9 **Write a sentence for each of the words underlined**
but this time use the word with another of its meanings.
The first one has been done for you.

1 I heard the <u>band</u> playing in the park.
 I put an elastic band around the papers.

2 Janet thought the price of the handbag very <u>dear</u>.
3 David did a <u>lap</u> around the track in four minutes.
4 Ken carried the <u>box</u> into the store.
5 The boys gave an <u>account</u> of the accident
 to the policewoman.
6 I wrote my name in <u>capital</u> letters.
7 Brian was able to <u>duck</u> as the ball came towards him.
8 The farmer drove the sheep into the <u>fold</u>.

10 **Read this poem, then answer the questions.**

How doth the little crocodile
Improve his shining tail,
And pour the waters of the Nile
On every golden scale.

How·cheerfully he seems to grin
How neatly spreads his claws,
And welcomes little fishes in,
With gently smiling jaws.
> *Lewis Carrol*

1 Who wrote the poem?
2 Suggest a title for the poem.
3 The word 'little' is an adjective.
 Make a list of three other adjectives
 which occur in the poem.
4 The word 'crocodile' is a noun
 Make a list of three other nouns
 which occur in the poem.
5 A river is mentioned in verse one.
 Name the river.

11 **Letter writing.**
This advertisement appeared in the March edition
of a magazine called FRIENDSHIP.

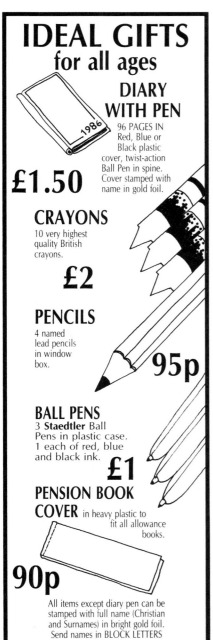

IDEAL GIFTS
for all ages

DIARY WITH PEN
£1.50

96 PAGES IN Red, Blue or Black plastic cover, twist-action Ball Pen in spine. Cover stamped with name in gold foil.

CRAYONS
10 very highest quality British crayons.
£2

PENCILS
4 named lead pencils in window box.
95p

BALL PENS
3 **Staedtler** Ball Pens in plastic case. 1 each of red, blue and black ink.
£1

PENSION BOOK COVER
in heavy plastic to fit all allowance books.
90p

All items except diary pen can be stamped with full name (Christian and Surnames) in bright gold foil. Send names in BLOCK LETTERS please and PO/Cheque to:–

NORTHERN NOVELTIES.
41 Carpenter Road, Bradford BD3 5HJ

Despatched within 21 days. Orders from Irish Republic please add 50%.

Pretend you are to order
the following:

a red diary for a boy friend
a blue diary for a girl friend
a pension book cover for an old lady.

**Write a business letter
to NORTHERN NOVELTIES
making your order and giving them
all the information they will require.**

12 **Describe how you would make
an emergency telephone call
to the POLICE.**

PUZZLE PAGE

THE A-Z PUZZLE (Part 2)

Complete this puzzle by filling in the missing letters.

1   To be unhappy
2   A gas, found in the air
3   A slanting line
4   A short written passage
5   Quarter of a circle
6   To speak well of somebody or something
7   A small planet which moves around a larger one
8   To go on land, or to enter a building
    where you have no right to be
9   A dreadful noise
10   A person who damages things
11   A cupboard for clothes
12   Short for Christmas
13   An evergreen tree
14   Turning from side to side as it goes along

#									
1	M			E	R			L	
2	N		T			G			
3	O	B			Q		E		
4	P		R			R		P	
5	Q			D			N		
6	R		C			M		N	
7	S	A			L				E
8	T	R		S			S		
9	U		R		R				
10	V	A		D					
11	W			R		B			
12	X	M							
13	Y		W						
14	Z		G	Z					